On Holy Ground

"The presence of God in our ordinary moments has an enduring quality of purpose as we reflect this gift into the world. Keith affirms, in a relatable context, this genuine understanding of vocation, that where we stand is holy ground; it is filled with the community of God, and we are included, carried, and equipped in that space. It is our invitation to respond. Thank you, Keith, for this beautiful revelation!"

—**WENDY DELCOURT**, licensed educator, author, and leadership coach

"*On Holy Ground* is a much-needed salve for a world searching for meaning and purpose. Keith shares a compelling and thought-provoking framework to integrate God's story with our story, calling us to a fuller and deeper understanding of who we are created to be. This book is a must-read for anyone searching for answers to some of life's most important questions: 'Who am I, how am I uniquely gifted, and who am I created and called by God to be?'"

—**DANA W. SCANNELL**, organizational psychologist and president, Scannell and Wight

"Over a long lifetime, I have known no one wiser than Keith Anderson. *On Holy Ground* is a resounding call to embrace what it means to be human and gift others with the face of God. There has never been an era where it is more important to rediscover the roots of our reason to be on this earth and to do so with wonder and joy. This profound and beautiful book will do far more than transform your life—it will set a course for a kinder world."

—**DAN B. ALLENDER**, founding president, The Seattle School of Theology and Psychology

"Keith Anderson's invitation to consider and embrace vocation is timely as we seek to make sense of our adult lives in this disorienting post-pandemic world. His storytelling, woven with his wise guidance, draws us in to discover our hunger for connection, belonging, identity, and purpose, opening us to the wonderful possibility of encountering Jesus and his companioning way with us. *On Holy Ground* provides us with much-needed wisdom and companionship on the journey."

—**ROBERT LOANE**, president, VantagePoint3 Ministries

"We probably don't need another book that helps us find a godly career, but we definitely need help exploring the way of life God is calling us to. In this book, Keith Anderson shares the wisdom of a lifetime helping young and old (including me) discover what the way of Jesus looks like in every area of their lives. I hope you join the conversation with him."

—**ROD REED**, vice president of Southeast region, CEO Forum

On Holy Ground

Finding Your Story of Identity,
Belonging, and Sacred Purpose

Keith R. Anderson
Foreword by Linda L. Schubring

CASCADE *Books* • Eugene, Oregon

ON HOLY GROUND
Finding Your Story of Identity, Belonging, and Sacred Purpose

Copyright © 2025 Keith R. Anderson. All rights reserved. Except for brief quotations in critical publications or reviews, no part of this book may be reproduced in any manner without prior written permission from the publisher. Write: Permissions, Wipf and Stock Publishers, 199 W. 8th Ave., Suite 3, Eugene, OR 97401.

Cascade Books
An Imprint of Wipf and Stock Publishers
199 W. 8th Ave., Suite 3
Eugene, OR 97401

www.wipfandstock.com

PAPERBACK ISBN: 979-8-3852-1921-6
HARDCOVER ISBN: 979-8-3852-1922-3
EBOOK ISBN: 979-8-3852-1923-0

Cataloguing-in-Publication data:

Names: Anderson, Keith R., author.
Title: On holy ground : finding your story of identity, belonging, and sacred purpose / Keith R. Anderson; foreword by Linda L. Schubring.
Description: Eugene, OR: Cascade Books, 2025. | Includes bibliographical references.
Identifiers: ISBN 979-8-3852-1921-6 (paperback) | ISBN 979-8-3852-1922-3 (hardcover) | ISBN 979-8-3852-1923-0 (ebook)
Subjects: LCSH: Intimacy (Psychology)—Religious aspects—Christianity. | Vocation—Christianity. | Identity—Christianity.
Classification: BV4501.3 A53 2025 (paperback) | BV4501.3 (ebook)

VERSION NUMBER 09/08/25

Unless otherwise noted, Scripture quotations are taken from The New Revised Standard Version, copyright© 1989, Division of Christian Education of The National Council of Churches of Christ in the United States of America. Used by permission. All rights reserved.

Scripture quotations marked (The Message) are taken from The Message, Copyright© by Eugene H. Peterson, 2002. Used by permission of NavPress. All rights reserved.

Scripture quotations marked (New International Version) are taken from the *Holy Bible, New International Version,* °New International Version Copyright©1973, 1978, 1984, by International Bible Society Used by Permission of Zondervan Publishing House. All Rights Reserved.

Scripture quotations from the Authorized (King James) version, Rights in the Authorized Version in the United Kingdom are vested in the Crown. Reproduced by permission of the Crown's patentee, Cambridge University Press.

Excerpts from *Hannah Coulter* © by Wendell Berry, 2004, reprinted by permission of the author and publisher, Counterpoint Press.

Excerpts from *Jayber Crow: The Life Story of Jayber Crow, Barber of the Port William Membership as Written by Himself* © by Wendell Berry, 2000, reprinted by permission of the author and publisher, Counterpoint Press.

Excerpts from *A Place in Time* © by Wendell Berry, 2012, reprinted by permission of the author and publisher, Counterpoint Press.

Excerpts from *Standing by Words* © by Wendell Berry, 2011, reprinted by permission of the author and publisher, Counterpoint Press.

Excerpts from *Written by Himself* © by Wendell Berry, 2000, reprinted by permission of the author and publisher, Counterpoint Press.

Godspeed: The Pace of Being Known ©. Used by Permission of the author and the Godspeed Project, livegodspeed.org.

"A Blessing for After" © by Jan Richardson from *Circle of Grace: A Book of Blessings for the Seasons*, 2015, reprinted by permission, janrichardson.com.

Excerpts from *So Much More: An Invitation to Christian Spirituality* © by Debra Rienstra, 2003. Used by permission.

For my grandchildren:
"I watch them grow, they'll learn much more than I'll ever know."
May your lives be filled with big questions and worthy dreams
as you set out to follow Jesus as the beloved of Abba.

Benjamin Carl White, Andrew Robert White, Samuel Marcelius
Anderson, Luke Torsten Anderson, Sloane Avery Anderson,
Laine Riley Anderson, Zachary Charles Anderson

ἐν ὄνομα Ιησους

Contents

Foreword: Your Sacred Story by Linda L. Schubring | xi
Introduction: Invitation to a Conversation | xiii

1 It's Not on Your Resume | 1
2 Does God Believe in You? Not a Typo—It's a Real Question | 10
3 Wait, What Did You Say, Lord? I Had Other Plans | 20
4 What If the Song Has It Wrong? What If This World Is My Home? | 30
5 Get Used to Different; We Call It the Kingdom of God | 39
6 God Comes to You Disguised as Your Life | 50
7 Who Holds the Pen that Writes Your Story? | 60
8 If You Knew All of My Story . . . | 69
9 Heartbreak and Shipwrecks | 77
10 Seriously God, the Church? Is That the Best You Could Do? | 86
11 In the Rearview Mirror: Learning to Read Backward | 95
12 Perspective at 14,410 Feet | 103

A Word After: What's Next? | 112
Appendix | 115
Bibliography | 117

Foreword
Your Sacred Story

ONE DAY IN THE cafeteria during my sophomore year of college, I walked through the sea of students carrying my tray. I was interrupted by Keith passing by: "Hartzell, I think I need to get to know you." He smiled and kept walking with his dining companions.

My first thought was shock that the campus pastor knew my name. Maybe he knew I played volleyball. Whatever it was, he saw something in me and called me to attention. I'm not sure we met until later that year, but in our meetings in the three decades since, I have been pushed, challenged, and loved. Keith is one of the balcony people who interrupts my life with encouragement, admonishment, abundance, and need.

Then Keith asked me to read this book. The world needs lived wisdom and people bold enough to model the way. Keith's courage to share his sacred journey reveals the mysteries of what has made him such an effective mentor, guide, and teacher over the years.

The book is a compilation of Keith's formation, information, and reformation. Keith wrings out his lived wisdom from his own story and his spiritual companions. He inspires you to find the grounding he found in community, his loved ones, his experiences, and the Bible. Then, he invites you to live your life and let it teach you something.

There is a deep hunger in leaders today. I hear longing in many conversations I have as a leadership consultant and executive coach. I've finally learned that longing is part of what it means to be human. No matter one's faith tradition or orientation, those seeking wisdom will never stop looking. Those desiring to uncover their sacred purpose will forever be on an adventure. We can go farther or deeper if we trust the guides and teachers who model the way and light our path.

Foreword

For three decades, Keith's voice shaped mine. I read and listened to the mystics, artists, and wanderers he recommended and referenced in this book. I listened to Keith's sermons both preached and lived. Then, I stepped out and lived mine. I was mentored well. A leisurely read-through, *On Holy Ground* feels like being mentored by Keith.

If you've longed for an expansive view of Jesus and the way of love, this is the book for you. If you've longed to glean some wisdom from someone with bumps, bruises, accomplishments, and accolades, this work is for you. In Keith's magnum opus, he invites you to his table for a chat. Imagine holding a nice warm beverage and listening to his thoughts and questions. Linger long enough and you'll hear your life speak. You won't be indoctrinated, but you might be healed.

The world needs this book. I did.

—Dr. Linda L. Schubring (aka "Hartzell")

Introduction
Invitation to a Conversation

IT WAS A CONVERSATION to remember. Linda was about twenty-five, an alum and now in her professional work in higher education. I was her mentor, about twice her age—and I am a wrestler. Not in the world of athletics, although I tried unsuccessfully as a seventy-nine-pound freshman in high school. No, I wrestle with life, spirituality, faith, and in this case, vocation and sacred purpose. I turned to her and called her the name I always use, "Hartzell, what should I do with my life?" She gulped, I think, laughed out loud, and said, "I'm supposed to ask you those questions. You're supposed to know. I'm supposed to ask you."

But we do know, don't we? If you have life and breath, you're searching too. Maybe you don't wrestle in the ways I do, but you are on the same journey—an ongoing life expedition to find out who you are and what you're called to do, the journey of vocation and sacred purpose, it may be called. We're all trying to sort that out because none of us has sorted it once and for all. We continually search for meaning as new conditions and circumstances emerge. Another way to talk about sacred purpose is that we don't arrive at all the answers at twenty-five, fifty, or seventy-four. The ache to know answers to these large questions is itself so big that it takes a lifetime. We may never find the "answers" but we can find our own ways to traverse the terrain of our story. Our deepest human longing is to find identity, meaning, and what I call sacred purpose. *So, welcome to a conversation about our most essential human needs: to find how our identity is formed, where we belong, and what our purpose is through the stages of life.*

I am aware that we are different, each of us. Your story is yours, not mine. Your history and background are different. Where and how you center your life may be very different from me. My life is centered where my

Introduction

faith is rooted—in the Scriptures of the New Testament and the Old Testament. Scripture provides many markers for my story that you'll learn if you turn the page and read on. You may find my commitment of faith in Jesus hard to understand. It is a particularity of who I am and how I have found my own life of sacred purpose. But my story is not the meta-story for anyone else. You need not become what I am, but you are invited to read what is something of a memoir of my story of sacred purpose. I write for all those who want to listen to their life as story to find the animating movement of sacred purpose. I write as a follower of Jesus, unashamed of my faith though I am sometimes embarrassed by Christians, frequently by myself.

Perhaps you will find familiarity with some moment of my story or in the biblical narratives I will retell. Perhaps you'll be inspired by those I gathered as my guest list of thoughtful writers and artists. I invite you to listen and ask your questions. Bring yourself to this book in any way you are able. That's how we learn best, after all, isn't it?

I have wrestled with questions you might bring to a book such as this. I have not *arrived* anywhere except somewhere along the path. Faith is not my native tongue. Spirituality, the life of the spirit within, has puzzled me, confused me, and fulfilled me. God has been . . . well, God. Sometimes more mystery than clarity. Sometimes seemingly more absent or silent than present. But along the way, I've had moments when I realized I was in on a conversation that started with someone other than me. Sometimes I've had the certainty that my very human faith changed the arc of my life. Or more accurately, God's love for me changed the arc of my life. What my story offers, perhaps, is a structure that may give you a context for your own journey on this pilgrimage of sacred purpose.

One thing I find at work in you, me, and the entire cast of biblical people is a shared human hunger for connection, belonging, identity, and purpose. And I have found all of these in a life of companionship with Jesus through the Holy Spirit. It's the way God guides us toward wholeness in everything we're up to in our lives—successes and failures, faith and, yes, doubt and questions. I don't know how those words will sound to you, perhaps vague or outside of your experience: "The Holy Spirit is the presence of Jesus since his death and resurrection." The Holy Spirit has been sent by Abba Father to help us pray, empower us, guide us, convict us of sin, give us strength, boldness and spiritual gifts. *Abba* is an Aramaic word Jesus used for God. It is an intimate familial term sometimes translated "Daddy." It may be helpful to remember that God is also identified as maternal: "As

Introduction

a mother comforts her child, so I will comfort you; you shall be comforted in Jerusalem" (Isaiah 66:13).

I am sadly aware not all of us experienced paternal relationships as caring, attentive, loving, or even honorable. That's the tragic reality of human fathers, but Jesus uses his word for God based on *his* relationship, not ours, whether helpful and tender or harmful or absent. How God is as Father is not an equivalent of our own fathers. In truth God as Father is meant to illuminate the best of fatherhood. We are meant to remember: Jesus is our best living picture of God.

Mystery seems to surround our understanding of the Holy Spirit. So, I turn back to Jesus' own words to clarify. "I have said these things to you while I am still with you. But the Advocate, the Holy Spirit whom the Father will send in my name will teach you everything and remind you of all that I have said to you" (John 14:25–26). The Holy Spirit, like Jesus himself, can be your teacher. The curriculum is Jesus. The Spirit testifies and points to Jesus and draws your attention toward life in him. Our role to play in this relationship is clear: we are learners, students of Jesus through the Spirit. As you learn more of Jesus you can be sure the Holy Spirit has been at work. Your task is to ask questions honestly and then to pay attention not only for answers but for images of Jesus given to you by the Spirit. As students we learn not only as we take notes from "the teacher" but from our questions, the conversations in our own minds and spirits, from other students, from textbooks, and always from listening to what may be revealed.

Sharon Daloz Parks asks a brilliant question in the classrooms where she has taught. "What did you hear yourself saying as I was speaking?" This is truthful, it seems to me: writers write with an intention of some sort and readers pay attention to the author's words with their own filtered curiosity, i.e., they find their own meaning. I welcome that experience for you as you read with your own thoughts and questions in mind and heart. I offer this book as an invitation to listen to your own story as you eavesdrop on my thoughts, ideas, and story, listening to find "whispers from afar" on this sacred journey. I pray there will be moments like one that Frederick Buechner described. "When a door opened somewhere that let the future in . . ."[1] because any conversation about vocation or calling is always a glimpse into the future, is it not?

We will explore the terrain of vocation and sacred purpose. It is an invitation to see your vocation as spirituality lived everywhere that you live.

---

1. Buechner, *Room Called Remember*, 20.

Introduction

It is holy ground because Abba is present wherever we journey. We can be even more explicit: every place is holy ground. There are desecrated places to be sure, where human violence, greed, and disregard has done its worst, but take these words with you as you read: every place is holy ground. That makes all of life an exploration into spirituality at a deep level. Learning to read what's going on deep underneath the surface in your story is itself a spiritual practice. I invite you to join me in asking questions that may surface from deep below. You might be surprised by what you hear.

Bono is one of those artists whose spirituality has surprised and instructed me. He gives an important place to begin: "Stop asking God to bless what you're doing. Find out what God's doing. It's already blessed."[2] I say, stop looking to find yourself blessed, you already are blessed because you are loved with an irrepressible love by the creator. If you can't believe that yet, I pray you will know it differently as you read with listening ears and a curious heart. I pray you will see yourself as I know God sees you: beloved, worthy, and capable, invited to participate in something larger than yourself.

The search for sacred purpose doesn't belong only to the young, but to all of us of whatever age. You may be young like my grandchildren, in your forties or fifties like my children, or you may be "seasoned" like my peers who don't believe in retirement but prefer the notion that we are redeployed for our next season of fidelity to Jesus. I don't ask the question of purpose exclusively of young people; it is a dynamic, sometimes changing, always essential quest for all ages. I have a strong conviction that your active search for sacred purpose is worth the effort because we adult learners learn best as we ask good questions, practice good listening, and show up ready to learn.

I am not writing a scholarly treatise on the history of vocation. I am not writing a career planning and placement manual. Discernment of vocation can lead to career planning, but it must begin with *the starting place*: a living relationship *with* Jesus. I write out of my own story as a kind of memoir because the most personal and particular stories are, in fact, a portal to the most universal. I hope my story will help you read your story as a living journal of your journey thus far. Questions are valued company on this journey. It turns out that faith and questions are not antithetical. Jesus invited questions and welcomed doubters, as well as those of strong faith. To have convictions doesn't mean you cannot ask questions of God. If you

---

2. Bono, National Prayer Breakfast Speech, 2006.

Introduction

don't believe that, read the Psalms. You'll find that Israel didn't hesitate to raise their questions to Yahweh. I'll let Wendell Berry's words speak for me:

> *It may be that when we no longer know what to do,*
> *we have come to our real work,*
> *and that when we no longer know which way to go*
> *we have come to our real journey.*
> *The mind that is not baffled is not employed.*
> *The impeded stream is the one that sings.*[3]

Vocation was not what I thought it was when I started studying the Bible: it is not merely an individual's search for a job or career. I discovered many biblical teachings that pointed me to *a spirituality of vocation*, not career discernment. I became convinced that we have limited our decision-making on the future to pragmatic questions: What are my natural talents? Is this the time to retire? Should I take the job and move across the country? All useful until you remember there is *Another* with whom you make an adventurous journey. Better questions are possible, are they not? *Whom* will I be to others? *How* will I be toward others? How do I find my way to a "way of life" with coherence and adventure, curiosity and direction? What "calls" or "draws" me in my life? How do I live into what I have been given? It turns out that a spirituality of vocation invites us to live attentively to our best story, together. What are the pivotal moments in my story that evoke a pathway for me to find sacred purpose in my life? How can I make a difference in my world and in our world? What moves me "toward . . ." and what moves me "away from . . ."? For whom is my sacred purpose intended?

What I hope you will hear in this conversation is how to keep an open channel with others and with our Abba. You know what happens when you pick up a headset and tune in to your device. It may start with static—just noise—and then may become garbled sound with occasional words coming through, perhaps even too loud to hear what is trying to be spoken until you find harmony of meaning, or at least clarity of words. And then, it turns out we may find an animating narrative for our lives. I'll say it again. In my story, the questions, the search, and the journey have become as important as identifying a map for my life. I have experienced the monumental power of questions that can form us spiritually and animate our souls.

I welcome that experience for you as you read with your own thoughts and questions in mind and heart. I offer this book as an invitation to listen to your own life as you eavesdrop on my thoughts, ideas, and story,

3. Berry, *Standing by Words*, 97.

listening to find "whispers from afar," on his sacred journey. I pray there will be moments like one that Frederick Buechner described, "When a door opened somewhere that let the future in . . ."[4] because any conversation about vocation or calling is always a glimpse into the future, is it not?

Context matters, especially as we set out to take seriously our search for sacred purpose. There can be little debate about the divided state of our culture today. Right/left, conservative/progressive, MAGA/traditionalist, in/out, inclusive/exclusive, us/them, we/they. When we accept such extreme dichotomies as normative, we see life as perpetually conflicted and views contested. God is for *us, our side, our team, our tribe, our politics* and thus *not for them,* anyone and everyone we define as *"other."* Everywhere we look, we tend to see others and are threatened by them. In such a culture, anxiety, worry, and fear become the bread of everyday life. Our vocabulary loses words like *we and us, compassion and mutual respect, discourse and hospitality, welcome and love.* Instead, we speak of the weaponization against the other, even if they happen to live across the street or down the hall. Our altered vocabulary is overtaken by words like *distance, contempt, disrespect, mistrust, vilification, dismissiveness,* and *violence.* It becomes the rhetoric of vitriol and too frequently straight-out hate speech.

Where is "sacred purpose" to be found in a culture so rigidly divided, angry, fearful, and plotting our next move against "the other"? I contend that sacred purpose is essential for the healing and preservation of a culture that seems to be at war with itself. When we know our identity as the beloved of God, our lives begin to take on practices urgently needed today: compassionate hospitality, dialogue and discourse with "the other, and living to the glory of God. Today, I see hunger for purpose everywhere as we attach ourselves to causes, political parties, cultural and social identities, and broken relationships, personal and social. God's intentions for us call us to seek the kingdom of God as we participate in God's purpose in the face of issues so charged and divisive as they are today—including race, inclusion/exclusion, violence, trauma, and myriad ways in which we dismiss, demean, and displace others. It is time for a radical re-imagination of familiar ideas of vocation and purpose; not just "who am *I* "but "who are *we* "under the Lordship of Jesus?" We are not the first generation to live in such disarray but this is our time, our moment, our opportunity. There is a great adventure ahead for those who commit to restore, unify, heal, redeem, reconcile, repair, and

---

4. Buechner, *Room Called Remember,* 20.

Introduction

rebuild. If you're up for the adventure, you'll need to set loose your imagination, faith, and hope. And always, your greatest gift: love.

I always love the feel of the salt breeze as I allow my senses to enjoy the waters of Puget Sound, just a mile away from my home. Maybe because we live in a Navy town, I love to watch movies of naval exploration and adventure. There is something of a summons to adventure in that same spirit of exploration, anticipation, and the risk of setting forth on this expedition. We join the movement with others likewise curious to find sacred purpose as we read our life as story. We will not discern sacred purpose sitting in port or safely ensconced in the harbor. I remember the first time I went salmon fishing on the Pacific Ocean. We were eight miles from shore and all we could see in any direction was ocean, sky, and waves that rocked our craft until the sound of three feet of fishing line began to whir as my first-ever salmon was hooked and tried its best to get free. There is adventure in joining a movement that also invites learning, growth, and exploration. Jesus was direct and clear: "Follow me."

1

It's Not on Your Resume

You may have heard it said that vocation is primarily about creating an award-winning resume. I'd like to change that: Vocation is finding your sacred purpose in the world through a living relationship with Jesus.

WE SETTLE TOO OFTEN for small questions that limit our curiosity rather than opening us to something more. Sometimes, however, we find large questions that move us by the raw energy and honesty of their words. "Tell me what it is you plan to do with your one wild and precious life."[1] Do you have an answer for the poet Mary Oliver? Her words evoke a large image of life that is anything but predictable and boring. Her question is an evocative place to begin to think about a spirituality of vocation and sacred purpose. You can see that she doesn't limit her question to something like, "What job are you planning to get?" or "What kind of career will satisfy your soul?" No, she starts with something more profound: a worldview of life as wild and precious. Therefore, we can gather up our tools to search for this hidden treasure with thoughtfulness and discernment. I love her question specifically for its starting place: Your life is precious, you have value, you are worthy, you have capacity to listen, imagine, and find your sacred purpose.

1. Oliver, *New and Selected Poems*, 94.

On Holy Ground

What will you do with that? No one can answer that for you, no book on sacred purpose will answer this curious summons. Such a question is not answered on your resume but by living your answer.

My battle with vocation began in an unexpected declaration heard on South Morgan Street in Chicago. When I was about ten, with us grandchildren and our parents squeezed into Grandpa and Grandma Liljedahl's bungalow on the far South Side. Grandma declared from her wheelchair, gesturing at me, "This one—the red-headed little boy will be the preacher." At ten. It was a crushing blow to my aspirations to play second base with Ernie Banks at first. It was like a death sentence for a ten-year-old boy. A preacher? Really? Please, Grandma, pick someone else. I set out to prove her wrong—my beloved grandmother. This one who spoke what she called "broken English." To this day I feel emotional when I hear someone from Sweden speak in that accented English. But I couldn't let her prediction go, or I should say, it wouldn't let me go.

Wendell Berry wrote, "The significance and ultimately the quality of the work we do is determined by our understanding of the story in which we are taking part."[2] The meaning of his words is dramatic. *The story we claim as our own will shape everything.* We become, to a large extent, that to which we pay attention. It's another way of saying we are people who care about certain things that shape our identity. Ask any Seattle Seahawks fan or someone with a golden retriever. These days, ask what political party they support and you'll also discern their identity. Our story is a patchwork of values, experiences, loyalties, and relationships. We are shaped as people most profoundly if we claim Jesus' story as our own. After all, Jesus' mission was to reveal God to us and, at the same time, to open our eyes to our identity. It's both simple and complex: Simple, because Jesus called us to childlike faith in Abba, Father. If I know God as Abba, I realize I am called into a living relationship that will inform, form, and transform everything. It's complex, because it is a lifelong way of life, a companionship through all of life.

Choose your own metaphor: a canvas on which to paint images and bring beauty, a blank page on which to write your story, the turn of a page to a new calendar that will be filled with your days and nights. Some suggest meaning comes when we see our life as precious as a work of art. Whichever metaphor you choose, keep an eye on this one thing: you are called, first and foremost, by God to life, life, and more life. My intention is to describe a spirituality that reverberates with gratitude for the gift of

---

2. Berry, "Christianity and the Survival of Creation," 8.

life and doesn't settle for anything less than an engaged way of being in the world that has purpose, belonging, and vocation.

I didn't think of myself as "called" until my early twenties. Those who knew themselves to be *called* were all church employees who said with reverence, "I was called . . ." I was not. I just went to school and church, worked my jobs, counted the days to graduation, and applied to college. Finding my sacred purpose wasn't in my vocabulary, let alone my thinking. I was doing alright. I was not preparing for a life or a career and certainly had no sense of call. "The future was coming to me, but I had not so much as lifted a foot to go to it."[3] Until college, I had carefully tucked away Grandma's prophetic word for my life's purpose. In time, I discovered that I *had* been called, but not to what I wanted; to my surprise, I *was* called as a pastor. What I had not anticipated was the creative movement of God. I had much to learn about the meaning of being called.

VOCARE: VOCATION OR CALLING

In Latin, the word for vocation is *vocare*, or *vocatio* as a noun. It means *to call* or even *shout* and has a background meaning as a *voice*. In Greek the equivalent word is *kaleo*, which literally means "crying out for a purpose." It also means called to be given a task (Matthew 24:14, Luke 19:13).[4] We can hear the summons of God and either accept it or reject it, listen to it or be deaf to it. God offers a task that is of use in the world. And always the call is to come and enjoy his fellowship, hospitality, and the joy and fullness of being a guest of God.[5]

In the Protestant Reformation, Martin Luther argued that vocation was not just for clergy but for all. There are, of course, numerous types of call in Scripture: there is a call to salvation (an effectual call), but also a call of God's direct involvement in our lives at times of need (a providential call). We are also equipped by the Spirit for a charism or spiritual gift (a charismatic call) and then finally to what most think of as our call to a job or even a career (occupational call).[6] It is evident that God is busy, engaged in saving, moving, equipping, and sending us to lives of compassionate service. The Swiss theologian Karl Barth used a compelling phrase to describe

---

3. Berry, *Jayber Crow*, 71.
4. Barclay, *Kaleo*.
5. Barclay, *Kaleo*.
6. Peacore, "Vocation and the Christian Life."

our part in this: we have "the freedom of obedience"[7] to use all that we have been given in fidelity to our particular call and context.

There is something of mystery, drama, and adventure in the thought that someone has a role to play in how we will spend your days and nights. If vocation merely means "*a job*" then *calling* is something more like "coming near a sleeping large animal." Wendell Berry, speaking of the end of a school day at his fictional Port William, writes, "When school let out, something burst loose and streamed forth in a cataract of motions and sounds: voices calling, shouting, singing, laughing, teasing, arguing."[8] To be called by God is an invitation to engage in a love story as energized as that moment when school lets out.

This spirituality takes us into the context of terms that have been used and misused over many years. *Vocation* sounds like a job but in a biblical context it is a summons to a relationship. It is not only about jobs or paychecks; it is about all of our life. *Calling* sounds like something for clergy but in a biblical context it is a summons to a relationship *for all*. *Vocational discernment* sounds like career planning but in a biblical context it is a summons to a way of living with sacred purpose through a living relationship with Jesus. I hope to have us return to this starting place with crucial questions. What is the true vocation of my life? How do we "learn" Jesus in a way that leads us back to the core relationship with him described in the Gospels? How do we practice our sacred purpose in the context of today's divided culture? Some of our most important teachers will be the cloud of witnesses whose stories reside in Scripture. They form a community of teachers who offer formative, redemptive, and missional learning for all. They are sometimes the very people we are too busy to let speak.

I know that some of this talk about "spirituality" will not sound familiar to everyone. Think of Christian spirituality where the goal is "learning from Jesus Christ how to live my life as He would live my life if He were me."[9] That makes Jesus the starting place, the Scriptures a living source, and curiosity a necessary practice. Spirituality is learning to pay attention to the presence of God in everything. We often get drawn in by questions rather than answers, curiosity rather than certitude. If that word, *spirituality*, still strikes you as vague, fuzzy, or merely metaphorical, read Eugene Peterson.

---

7. Doperbeck, *Barth Through a Glass Darkly*, 1.
8. Berry, *Jayber Crow*, 89.
9. Willard, "Spirituality Made Hard."

It's Not on Your Resume

He is one of our best teachers about spirituality because he was a careful reader of Scripture and student of Jesus.

> Jesus keeps our feet on the ground, attentive to children, in conversations with ordinary people, sharing meals with friends and strangers, listening to the wind, observing the wildflowers, touching the sick and wounded, praying simply and unselfconsciously. Jesus insists that we deal with right here and now, in the place we find ourselves and with the people we are with. Jesus is God right here and now.[10]

Scripture, spirituality, and sacred purpose form an ecosystem, interdependent, interconnected, and living. In the language of biology, this is considered to be symbiotic, an interaction between living organisms. Within the image of an ecosystem, we understand that *Scripture (the living word) points us to Jesus (the incarnate Word) who calls us to sacred purpose, (a living relationship of following Jesus), at our own altars in the world, for all of our lives.*

Paul, summarizes the biblical view of vocation: "It's in Christ that we find out who we are and what we're meant to do" (Ephesians 1:11, The Message). *Don't miss what Paul wants you to hear.*

- You are "*called to belong to Jesus Christ*" (Romans 1:6). Nothing yet about a job or career but something more precious: a relationship of belonging. Biblical spirituality begins there: we belong to Jesus. Belonging is perhaps our most essential human need.

- "God is faithful: by him you were *called into the fellowship of his Son*, Jesus Christ, our Lord" (1 Corinthians 1:9). The call to life is initiated from God in Jesus. We are not only called alone, as a soloist, but together as an orchestra in sacred song. Vocation is not only about who *I* am, but who *we* are in relationships of belonging and communion.

- "I press on toward the goal for the *prize of the heavenly call* of God in Jesus Christ" (Philippians 3:14). Once called, we are summoned to "press on" with vigorous energy to meet our life's goal. We are not passive bystanders to this spirituality of vocation.

- "Therefore, if anyone is in Christ, the new creation has come: The old has gone, the new is here! All this is from God, who reconciled us to himself through Christ *and gave us the ministry of reconciliation*"

---

10. Peterson, *Christ Plays*, 33–34.

(2 Corinthians 5:17–18, emphasis mine). What is this call to reconciliation? Simply put, people can be made right as they accept their identity as the beloved of God.

- "I therefore, the prisoner in the Lord, beg you to *lead a life worthy of the calling* to which you have been called . . ." (Ephesians 4:13). We are not the source or starting place but we become partners with God as we seek to live into the mystery of our call.

- "For those God foreknew he also predestined *to be conformed to the image of his Son* . . . And those he predestined he also called; those he called, he also justified; those he justified, he also glorified" (Romans 8:29–30). *Why* are we called? That we may be justified (set right with God) and sanctified (made holy for sacred purpose). *How* are we called? By grace we are given our identity as the beloved of God. *Who* calls us? By divine initiative alone, not dependent on human work, calling is the work of God alone.

- "But . . . God, who set me apart from my mother's womb . . . *called me by his grace* . . ." (Galatians 1:15, my emphasis). The call comes from God and most explicitly, from grace. What did Paul do as a result of God's gift of grace? He became the clearest voice for the centrality of Jesus in the mission of reconciliation, peace, and love. (See also 1 Corinthians 7:15.)

- "Let *each of you* lead the life that the Lord has assigned, to which God *called* you" (1 Corinthians 7:17, emphasis mine). *Everyone of us* is called or assigned.

- "All this is from God, who reconciled us to himself through Christ and gave us the ministry of reconciliation: that God was reconciling the world to himself in Christ, not counting people's sins against them. And *he has committed to us the message of reconciliation*" (2 Corinthians 5:18–19). It's breathtaking—can you feel it? We are given a ministry (sacred purpose) as agents of reconciliation. In solidarity with God's mission is our own mission of reconciliation.

Wendell Berry has captured my affection for his art as a writer, poet, and thinker. His work fills my soul with something I don't find elsewhere. He is a Kentucky farmer who has spent much of his life in an intersection between farming and writing. I am drawn especially to his novel, *Jayber Crow: The Life Story of Jayber Crow, Barber of the Port William Membership as Written by Himself.* I didn't expect a barber would captivate my interest and become a teacher to me, as Jayber, in fact, has done. He did not intend to become a barber but the work *found him*, an unexpected possibility for us all. Late in his years he looked back in reflection,

> Now I have had most of the life I am going to have, and I can see what it has been. I can remember those early years when it seemed to me, I was cut completely adrift, and times when, looking back at earlier times, it seemed I had been wandering in the dark woods of error. But now, it looks to me as though I was following a path that was laid out for me, unbroken, and maybe even as straight as possible, from one end to the other, and I have this feeling, which never leaves me anymore, that I have been *led*. I will leave you to judge the truth of that for yourself . . .[11]

But Jayber didn't stop there. He has more to say: He returned to his childhood home after years away and observed, "This is one of the doings I can tell you that I have learned: our life here is in some way marginal to our own doings, and our doings are marginal to the greater forces that are always at work."[12] We are asked by a vocation spirituality: Is there *an intention* to my life?

SOLI DEO GLORIA

Vocation is not one thing but many things . . . but there is a starting place called *Soli Deo Gloria*. "Do all to the glory of God" (1 Corinthians 10:23). We share a common vocation: to live to the glory of God. "For from him and through him and to him are all things. To him be the glory forever. Amen" (Romans 11:36). What that means shapes every moment of how we live life! We work for Jesus. Every one of us. You make art or music for God. You drive a truck or teach your class for God. You are an accountant for Jesus or a cook. The list is endless. Everything is for the glory of God. *Soli Deo Gloria*. It is the starting place of a biblical understanding of our sacred vocation. "I give thanks to you, O Lord my God, with my whole heart, and I will glorify your name forever" (Psalm 86:12). We have our vocation if we will receive it, to live all of life solely for the glory of God. It starts in daily practices of awareness, paying attention to the presence of God in all things,

---

11. Berry, *Jayber Crow*, 66.
12. Berry, *Jayber Crow*, 37.

including our very human selves, listening for a voice, seeking presence and knowing ourselves to be loved and finding our sacred purpose in the world.

We needn't look far to find a foundational holy purpose: "He has told you, O mortal, what is good; and what does the Lord require of you but to do justice, and to love kindness and to walk humbly with your God?"(Micah 6:8). And Paul wants us to be clear: God is glorified as we are formed into Christlikeness by the Holy Spirit. In fact, God is glorified as we love others as Christ loved us. "I pray that you have the power to comprehend with all the saints, what is the breadth and length and height and depth and to know the love of Christ that surpasses knowledge, so that you may be filled with all the fullness of God . . . The gifts he gave were . . . to equip the saints for the work of ministry, for building up the body of Christ, until all of us come to the unity of the faith and of the knowledge of the Son of God, *to maturity, to the measure of the full stature of Christ*" (Ephesians 3:18–19, 4:12–13, emphasis mine). Our vocation is ultimately to be made like Jesus in maturity and grow into the full stature of Christ loved by Abba. Jesus wanted his students to understand his teaching: "These words I speak to you are not mere additions to your life . . . They are foundation words, words to build a life on" (Luke 6:46, The Message). In Genesis we read, "Then God said, "Let us make humankind in our image, according to our likeness" (Genesis 1:26). We are created *imago dei*, in the image of God, and therefore capable of living to the glory of God.

CORAM DEO

We not only live *Soli Deo Gloria*, but *Coram Deo*, "before the face of God," or "in the presence of God's face." It literally means living where we are seen by Abba Father. That takes us from *thinking* about God to *living* what we believe and know. The essence of *Coram Deo* is to "live one's entire life in the presence of God, under the authority of God, to the glory of God."[13] It's a promise of presence with God. The psalmist asks, "Where can I go from spirit? Or where can I flee from your presence?" The answer in Psalm 137 is almost shocking. There is no place where we are apart from God. God is not detached from where and how we live. We live all parts of our life in the presence of God (*Coram Deo*) for a single purpose, (to bring honor and glory to God—*Soli Deo Gloria*). Your life becomes a benediction (good word) or a doxology (an expression of praise). "And whatever you do, in

13. Sproul, "What Does Coram Deo Mean?"

word or deed, do everything in the name of the Lord Jesus, giving thanks to God the Father through him" (Colossians 3:17). One of the catechisms of the church asked: "Why did God make you?" The answer is comprehensive: "to know, love, and serve God."

To follow Jesus, you adjust your line of sight to the horizon to seek first the kingdom of God, *Soli Deo Gloria*. When Jesus says, "Seek *first* the kingdom" he's saying "do this in *all* that you do." The difference it makes in how you approach your day is profound. My practice once was to get to the office early, take a quiet moment and pray for the scheduled and unscheduled events ahead. I could then walk into the day with receptivity for whatever God would send my way. At least on some days. To live *Soli Deo Gloria* may be as simple as finding one person to bless everyday. It may be grand and large acts but, for most of us, it is in the small, even mundane acts of blessing as we live intentionally every day to the glory of God.

Lloyd Ogilvie was a pastor whose final calling was as chaplain to the US Senate. His task was to pray at the start of each day for the Senate. Read this one aloud:

> Dear God, you have ordained that there is one decision we must make every day. It is the most crucial decision in the midst of all the other decisions we are called to make. We hear Elijah's challenge: "Choose for yourself this day whom you will serve," (Joshua 24:15). You have given us the freedom to choose whom we will serve today. We want to renew our decision to serve You as the only Lord of our lives. We know that without this decisive intentionality, we will drift into secondary loyalties. You entrust Your strength, gifts of leadership and vision onto those who start each day with a fresh decision to do everything for Your glory and according to your specific guidance. In the quiet of this moment, we make our decision to worship you with our work. You alone are our Lord and Savior. Amen.[14]

> Pause for reflection. We have one task each day, one decision to make: "choose you this day whom you will serve." Place these words in a place you see every day. This is how we live *Soli Deo Gloria*. Pause to make a renewed choice each day.

14. Ogilvie, "Senate Chaplain's Prayers."

2

Does God Believe in You?
Not a Typo—It's a Real Question

You may have heard it said that vocation begins as you understand your self-identity, capacities, and aspirations. I'd like to change that and say the starting place to understand vocation is to recognize your primary identity as the beloved of God.

AND THE LINES DANCE

ONE OF MY LIFE'S important teachers inspired the theme of this work. He was Dag Hammarskjöld, a Swede, the second secretary-general of the United Nations and a man of faith. His life was lived on the firing line of world history. He was honest about his questions and animated by his faith.

> Thou takest the pen—and the lines dance.
> Thou takest the flute—and the notes shimmer.
> Thou takest the brush—and the colors sing.
> So, all things have meaning and beauty in that
> space beyond time where Thou art.
> How then can I hold back anything from Thee?[1]

---

1. Hammarskjöld, *Markings*, 118.

Does God Believe in You? Not a Typo—It's a Real Question

A LOVE STORY WITH ABBA

Barbara Brown Taylor reflects on the "call" of the first disciples.

> This is not a story about us. This is a story about God and about God's ability not only to call us but to create us as people who are able to follow—able to follow because we cannot take our eyes off the one who calls us, because he interests us more than anything else in our lives, because he seems to know what we hunger for and because he seems to be food.

To be called, in her way of seeing it, then is a love story.

> If they [the apostles] did anything under their own power at all, it was simply that they allowed themselves *to fall in love.* Jesus showed up, they took one look at each other, and the rest was history. God acted and the disciples let their nets wash out to sea.[2]

Our experience can be the same: we see ourselves through the eyes of Abba, we see each other through the eyes of Abba, and we can't quite fully believe what we experience: Abba's eyes are full of love for me and you.

It may surprise you to learn that you are welcomed into a love story with Abba, who created you, knows you, dreams with you, and deploys you because Abba loves you with an irrepressible love. Not distant, detached, or impersonal but present, engaged, and relational, Abba's love is lifelong and integral to your story. We begin where we must as we listen faithfully to Scripture, with Abba's love revealed to us in Jesus' words. Whatever God intends for your life, it comes out of deep love and affection for you. Whatever God purposes for your purpose, it comes out of covenant love that started on day one of creation. Whatever God guides you toward was foreseen long before you began to find your way. "I know the plans I have for you," he said to Jeremiah and to each one of us. God's love is the initiating action in our pursuit of purpose.

Spirituality is reading the story God is writing in you. In love and with intention, God becomes present in your story and will move you toward sacred purpose. We start where Scripture starts, with God's intentions. Those words, easy as they are to type, are not easy for me to trust, which is why I needed Brennan Manning in my life. I hosted him for chapel, listened attentively to him, but as his sermon took momentum, I began to think about my responsibility as host *after* the sermon. I heard Brennan call for prayer

---

2. Taylor, *Home by Another Way*, 57.

so I bowed my head. And there it was, water on the floor, my shoes, and beside the chair. It startled me, to be truthful. I didn't remember bringing water into chapel that day. By this time, Brennan was asking us to imagine ourselves seated with Jesus who calls us by name, blesses us, and says, "You are the beloved of Abba, your father." I *felt* the words more than I heard them but something remarkable was taking place without my control—I felt the words because God's Spirit moved in my soul in ways that brought the unexpected flow of my tears. Do you understand? I wasn't *listening* but I *heard* the words. I wasn't paying attention but I felt the words move in me because I was hungry and longed for belonging. That day, God was there, beside me, and within me.

On my best days, I remember and feel my identity. On some days I live in doubt, hoping and waiting for faith to appear. I am not alone with doubt. It's part of faith. Of course, I long for faith everyday but honesty causes me to live in the movement between doubt and faith. "Lord I believe, help my unbelief" (Mark 9:24). On other days I need to be reminded who I am, the beloved of God. One verse to never forget: "Do not fear, for I have redeemed you. I have called you by name, you are mine. When you pass through the waters I will be with you . . ." (Isaiah 43:1–2). Though we may feel overwhelmed, we are never alone. Though we feel fear we are not abandoned but surrounded by and covered with an inexplicable love. "God loves you. God knows your name. Do not fear . . ."

Inner changes begin a process of redefining our identity and living with sacred purpose, which involves us in conversation with Abba, another word for prayer. "Prayer is us taking a chance against all odds and past history, [that] we are loved and chosen, and do not have to get it all together before we show up."[3] Bernard Lonergan wrote in words that we can sing as a doxology of praise and adoration: "All religious experience at its root is an experience of the unconditional and unrestricted being in love."[4] Because we are loved, these are given: identity, belonging, purpose, and worth.

In the upper room with Jesus, one student, John, understood this in a visceral way. "The disciple Jesus loved was reclining next to Jesus . . . He leaned back on Jesus' breast" (John 13:22, 25). What happened shows the difference between cognitive and relational knowing. John literally could hear and feel the heartbeat of Jesus. John knew Jesus to be "the human face of the

---

3. Lamott, *Help, Thanks, Wow*, 6.
4. Lonergan, "Growing in Faith."

God who is love."[5] Knowing himself to be loved was a formative moment in its rawest sense: he discovered sacred purpose for his life and became one of our best writers of Jesus' story and teaching. "Whoever remains in me with me in him bears fruit in plenty" (John 15: 4, The Message).

> Pause for reflection: "You are the beloved of God." Who in your life has shown you that precious fact? Who has denied that in your story? Do you know yourself as the beloved of God today? Do you feel it? What hinders you from knowing you are beloved?

You are the beloved of God. How can anyone say that? Because they read the Gospels and observe Jesus' treatment of people: it is our best evidence. How did he treat those he encountered? He told the truth and he showed compassion. The ones he critiqued most were the self-righteous, the religious, and the judgmental. Jesus shows us how God sees us. Can you believe these words: "I am the beloved of God"? "Being the beloved is our identity, the core of our existence. It is not merely a lofty thought, an inspiring idea, or one name among many. It is the name by which God knows us and the way He relates to us."[6] This is our story of origin: we were created to participate in God's intentions for the world. Sometimes Jesus explicitly added accountability: "Go and sin no more." Because you know yourself to be loved you are called to walk in faithful relationship (God's ways). Your primary identity was not self-constructed, it was given to you as you were created in the image of God, to reflect God to others. It is Abba's intention that we live in sacred purpose. In Mark's gospel, one of the first things Jesus says is utterly profound: "The kingdom of God has come near, repent, and believe in the good news" (Mark 1:15). "Change your life and believe the Message" (Mark 1:15, The Message). To repent is to turn from ... To believe is to turn toward. Repentance of sin is first—*we turn from*, i.e., we are going east and turn to go west, then *we turn toward*, we move in a new direction ... toward the direction of belief that will lead us to sacred purpose.

And there it is: *vocation is nothing less than companionship with Jesus through the Holy Spirit in loving response to Abba Father*. We're talking

---

5. Manning, *Abba's Child*, 124.
6. Manning, *Abba's Child*, 50.

about *all* of life and not merely one, two, or a handful of decisions to be made in a lifetime. We're talking about responding to being loved by Abba with amazement and adoration. Adoration begets adoration, calling begets response, vocation begets diligent faithfulness, a living relationship in which we read, listen, question, and respond. "Our primary calling as followers of Christ is by him, to him, and for him. First and foremost, we are called to Someone (God), not to something (such as motherhood, politics, or teaching) or to somewhere (such as the inner city or Outer Mongolia)."[7]

In Jesus, God came to humankind in a human body to bring redemption through relationship with him. He came first in the flesh and he comes now in the Spirit to bring life. In Jesus, God walked among us to bring us life through the irrepressible love that has always been the very nature of God. Does that sound too abstract or grandiose? This is the gift we most need, the gift we know we need but forget to pursue in our busyness with other things. God is available to each one of us—to you, whether you are just starting this journey or have traveled this road for decades. You don't need to be a spiritual giant, a monk, a biblical scholar, or even a leader. God promises to be present to you as you wait on the Lord, as you learn to listen, as you practice the discipline of attention. Julie Canlis says, "If you think you have to invoke the Spirit to enter your day, the good news is that the Spirit is already ahead of you. The entire created world is the Spirit's playground, as is your ordinary life. The Spirit's particular mission in your life is to draw you deeper and deeper into the new creation, which is another way of saying that the Spirit desires to draw you more deeply into life in Christ."[8]

William Barry explains: "We must school ourselves to pay attention to our experience of life in order to discern the touch of God or what Peter Berger calls the *rumor of angels*..."[9] Reading, listening, and seeing are ways we pay attention to the presence of God in our story. God shows up, seen or unseen, seen now or not seen until we look in the rearview mirror, but we are formed as we pay attention. Set aside your distractedness. Be. Here. Now. Sometimes we hear most clearly in times of solitude and reflective silence. Sometimes silence is enough.

You may have heard of Brother Lawrence, a monk, kitchen worker, and simple follower of Jesus who live from about 1614 to 1691. His book title is his message: *The Practice of the Presence of God.* What Brother

---

7. Guinness, *Call*, 31.
8. Canlis, *Theology of the Ordinary*, 56.
9. Barry, *God's Passionate Desire and Our Response*, 109.

Lawrence did all can do. No theological training nor any special theological views are needed for the blessed "practice" he recommended. No gorgeous churches, no stately cathedral, no elaborate ritual, could either make or mar it. A kitchen and an altar were as one to him; and to pick up a straw from the ground was as grand a service as to preach to multitudes. "The time of business," said he, "does not with me differ from the time of prayer . . ."[10]

Jesus' unrelenting message was his call to people to shift their center of gravity to the kingdom of God. He challenged them to see the kingdom of God in themselves, in their midst, in their neighborhood. Spirituality that is shaped by Jesus is a call to pay attention to the presence of God in everything. For Jesus there was single-minded obedience, a fearless, undaunted listening to the living word of Abba. And such words were never heard before Jesus spoke them. To his helplessly human band of ragamuffin students, he said what must have sounded more like a love letter than a lesson. "I've loved you the way my father has loved me. *Make yourselves at home in my love*" (emphasis mine). "If you keep my commandments you'll remain intimately at home in my love. That's what I've done—kept my Father's commands and made myself at home in his love" (John 15:9–10, The Message). When we know ourselves to be loved, there are limitless possibilities for our lives. When God seems more hidden than present, we do well to turn back to see how Jesus loved, healed, and restored in the particularity of his love. "Thy faith hath made thee whole" (Mark 5:34, KJV).

In the Synoptic Gospels, Matthew, Mark and Luke tell the story of a woman sick for twelve years with a disorder that made her unclean and an outcast from society. Her faith, however, was strong enough to brave a crowd as she lunged forward to touch the hem of Jesus' cloak. He felt power leave his body and insistently asked, "Who touched me?" She came forward and the most remarkable moment was an intimate word between Jesus and the woman who had undoubtedly been rejected by her own father and family. He spoke words of healing, "Your faith has made you well, go in peace, and be healed of your disease" (Mark 5:34). But there was more, another word spoken to a woman isolated from others, shunned by society, and excluded by her family. "Daughter." I can imagine her reply, 'I am no longer anyone's daughter." Undaunted, Jesus said, "Daughter, beloved child of God." For anyone who has felt discarded, unwanted, disregarded by people, let this word be one that echoes in your soul as it no doubt did for

---

10. Lawrence, *Practice of the Presence of God*, 7–8.

the woman some call Veronica as she felt intense, deep, and personal love. Daughter. My child. Beloved one.

Love can only be particular. I love landscapes in general, but I love Mt. Rainier in particular. I have hiked hundreds of miles with my family on that particular mountain. I have climbed to the summit at 14,410 feet. I feel at home when I walk those trails, smell the forest and meadow wildflowers. To live into a spirituality of vocation is to make yourself at home in the particularity of Abba's love and find your place in Abba's world. Linda Schubring asked a question I cannot ignore. "If someone could wrap you up in love, what would it change for your life and for our world?" It would give us sacred purpose for every day, rooting our identity in something large enough to give us meaning. It would fill the longing we all have to sort out identity, belonging, and hunger for sacred purpose.

What keeps us from moving home to God's love? We are preoccupied. The word means I am *occupied before* I get to whatever occupies me. It may be worry, anxiety, fear, guilt, distractions, grief, declining health, busyness, or even our dreams. What I hoped for at eighteen hasn't worked out, what now? God is already present. If you want to change the arc of your life, start there: believe the meaning of this biblical instinct: you are the beloved of God. Let Fleming Rutledge show you how.

> Maybe you are not up for considering global issues right now. Maybe you had a hard time just getting out of bed this morning. Maybe your marriage is on the rocks. Maybe someone you love is gravely ill. Maybe you are worried about your future. Maybe you are tired of the role you feel you have to play in order to measure up to somebody else's expectations. Maybe your faith is exhausted.
>
> Here's a message for you today. You are not saved by your spirituality or by anything else. You have been and you will be saved by God. The Holy Spirit of God is your friend. The Holy Spirit is the love of God reaching out for you when you are too depressed, or too angry, or too tired to reach out. The Holy Spirit is the power of God to set you on your feet when you feel you cannot stand up. Forget your own spirituality. We are talking about God today, the force that created the universe yet comes to you personally and intimately with an everlasting and unconditional love when you believe it or not.[11]

---

11. Rutledge, *Means of Grace*, 145–46.

Does God Believe in You? Not a Typo—It's a Real Question

BRENNAN MANNING

If you've never heard the unmistakable sound of his voice, timbre, and powerful rhetoric, you can find sermons on YouTube and understand why I miss it so much. To get just a taste of his thoughts on our identity, you can read these words from *Abba's Child: The Cry of the Heart of Intimate Belonging*. His consistent theme would sound like this: "My deepest awareness of myself is that I am deeply loved by Jesus Christ and I have done nothing to earn it or deserve it."

- "Let the great Rabbi hold you silently against His heart. In learning who He is, you will find who you are: Abba's child in Christ our Lord."
- "Define yourself radically as one beloved by God. This is the true self. Every other identity is illusion."
- "Our identity rests in God's relentless tenderness for us revealed in Jesus Christ."[12]

God's love is the starting place. "God is the center from which all of life develops."[13] To know your calling is to know that you are first and foremost the beloved of God. I wonder if you can believe that? I know my own struggles to accept my identity as one loved by God. It is the tragic sadness of so many in the church, this inability to believe we are loved because we are loved, nothing more. Brennan told me that a great majority of Christians do not have that experience of knowing themselves as the beloved of God. Jesus understood that and in one single sentence gave a universal summons: "Love one another the way I have loved you." (John 15:12, The Message).

Union with Jesus is where it all happens. You abide in Jesus. You make your heart a home for him. He makes his heart a home for you. This is where sacred purpose *begins*: with this love story of companionship with the living God through the presence of the Spirit. This is how sacred purpose *continues*: we know ourselves to be chosen, appointed, and sent. The lines dance, the notes shimmer, the colors sing. It is good poetry but an even better experience. "But God, who is rich in mercy, out of the great love with which he loved us, even when we were dead through our trespasses, made us alive together with Christ . . . For by grace, you have been saved through faith, and this is not your own doing, it is the gift of God . . ."

12. Manning, *Abba's Child*, 59.
13. Peterson, *Run With the Horses*, 96.

(Ephesians 2:5, 8). Finding your sacred purpose is a love story God is writing in your story. "If we do not know we are the beloved sons and daughters of God, we're going to expect someone in the community to make us feel special and worthy. Ultimately they cannot."[14]

WHERE DO YOU HEAR GOD'S VOICE?

If you're at the beginning or in the middle of an important decision, does it mean you leave your everyday world to pursue a mystical, monastic way of listening? Does it mean you need to find a seat in a cathedral so you can feel "spiritual" and "holy"? Both are valuable—yes, do that. But not because you can only listen for God's voice in a monastery or sanctuary. Not because you must leave your present setting in order to read what God's pen is writing. Do that only because it may help you to listen well. A better question is: how and where have you sensed God's voice *before*? Go there and read your story on familiar ground. I find that mowing a field is one of those places where I listen well. The motion, repetition, and being surrounded by the sweet smell of freshly mowed grass combine to give me my own cathedral in the pasture. Brennan often told me that our journey requires one persistent discipline: to show up. There is complexity to this, to be sure: we are not always given clear or definitive guidance. Sometimes we are left in a state of unknowing; what ought we do then? Show up. It's a good place to begin. It's step one. Where and how you read what God is writing in your story may be as individual as you are. Follow your own practices, but listen deeply in at least these ways:

- Listen to the mind and heart of God in *prayer*. Too busy? You will find it hard to discern God's intentions without the practice of listening prayer. Prayer takes many forms—ritual prayers, spontaneous, and personal prayers are often the daily form we most use. Formulated prayers including the Lord's Prayer give us an outline and structure that can be adaptive, personal, and passionate.

- Listen to the mind and heart of God as you read *Scripture*. Too distracted to read sacred text? Read it as a personal conversation with Abba.

---

14. Nouwen, *Wisdom for the Long Walk of Faith*, 115.

- Listen for the mind and heart of God in conversations with *spiritual friends, mentors, and elders.* God's words may come in a familiar human voice.

- Listen to *your experience of love* in your story: how have you known yourself loved and how do you practice loving others?

- *Work* is of course a major part of our lives as one of the ways God invites us to listen.

- *Suffering, pain, and trauma* are not always understood as ways God writes our story but the psalmist would disagree. "Yea, though I walk through the valley of the shadow of death, I will fear no evil, for thou art with me" (Psalm 23:1, KJV). Rather than fear what might be ahead, we are invited to pay attention to presence. We are not alone in suffering, pain, and trauma. Until we experience suffering existentially, we cannot understand the depths of our own humanity.

- *Loss* is common to our humanity. We prefer victories, wins, and successes, but loss is a great teacher of spirituality. Ask any athlete, they will say, "I learned most from my injury, losing the big game, or getting cut from the team." In the heart of the civil rights movement, a song became an iconic representation for the faith that empowered people to stay strong in the midst of loss: "We shall overcome . . . some day." Through Jesus we overcome loss, tragedy, and even oppression. Loss is one of our greatest teachers of spirituality and purpose.

Jesus sets the table for us in company with others. It is *our* story, the story of shared humanity in its beauty and brokenness. I discovered Thomas Merton, a mystic and social activist, when I was in my twenties. How could someone be both a contemplative and an activist, I wanted to know? He asked, "Who am I?" His answer says it all: "I am one loved by Christ."[15] Lived this way, our purpose becomes sacred purpose, our life a doxology of praise lived and not only spoken, and our identity a gift offered through the grace of Abba, our Father. Love is a catalyst for more love.

---

15. Finley, *Merton's Palace of Nowhere,* 96.

3

Wait, What Did You Say, Lord? I Had Other Plans

You may have heard it said that vocation is about you, your plans, and your aspirations. I want to change that: Vocation is listening for God's intentions for the world so that you may listen for your vocation in God's mind and heart.

I'M GLAD I WASN'T Jeremiah. He was young when God summoned him. God didn't ask him to start out easy and slow. God took him abruptly from the sidelines to the arena with a daunting mission. "Now the word of the Lord came to me saying, before I formed you in the womb, I knew you, and before you were born, I consecrated you, I appointed you a prophet to the nations" (Jeremiah 1:5). God spoke words of vocation to a young man and the drama began. It was not an experience for him alone. What if God has similar thoughts for you? How do you suppose young Jeremiah felt about this news? Like many of us, his immediate response was, "Wait, what did you say? Lord, I have other plans, what do you mean by this assignment?"

"Then Jeremiah said, "Ah, Lord God! Truly I do not know how to speak, for I am only a boy" (Jeremiah 1:6). It's always good to mount an excuse based on a lack of experience. How can I do this work, I'm too young or perhaps too old? It usually backfires, as it did for Jeremiah. "But the Lord said to me, 'Do not say, I am only a boy; for you shall go to all to whom I send you and you shall speak whatever I command you. Do not be afraid of them for I am with you to deliver you, says the Lord'" (Jeremiah 1:8). "Then the Lord put out his hand and *touched my mouth*; and the Lord said to me, "Now I have put words in your mouth . . ." (Jeremiah 1:9, emphasis mine).

Jeremiah was like Moses, who protested, "Who am I that I should go to Pharaoh, and bring the Israelites out of Egypt?" (Exodus 3:11). Both men were incredulous that God had such big intentions for them. Moses argued the call until God had enough. "No, go, and *I will be with your mouth.*" I am no longer surprised to see the response of those called by God—some are overwhelmed, some argue, some discount God's assessment of their readiness, and some few are receptive from the start, but the raw honesty of people like Jeremiah and Moses is evidence that God's call may be costly. It will ask something of your life to say yes. God spoke and touched their mouths, the very instrument they would need to be stewards of God's call. God touches not only our heart, but our mouth, hands, mind, will, and strength. No image is quite as tender, nor as intimate. God's touch is a sign of affirmation, empowerment, and companionship: "Jeremiah, I have equipped you for this work and I will not send you out alone. *My touch is upon you.*" As someone who has spent much of his life preaching and teaching, I have felt that touch upon my mouth too. Not every time, but often enough to know how Jeremiah's call transformed him from a hesitant young boy to a fierce prophet in some of the worst of times.

> Pause for reflection: What would it mean for you to have God touch your mouth, your mind, your plans, your dreams?

We follow Jesus by reading the story of our identity as the beloved of Abba as we move toward a transformed sacred purpose. You will see as you read ahead that our purpose is given first *in the intentions of God in Scripture*. Holy Scripture is not given merely for devotional or inspirational value, although we need that. Scripture invites us into a world of coherence, engagement, and integrity. "Thy will be done on earth as it is in heaven" is the animating principle for sacred purpose. Our part is to be bold and rigorous learners—learning both *about* Jesus (his way and his words) and *from* Jesus (through the Spirit). And then, like good artists, athletes, or apprentices, *we practice* what we have learned.

BIG QUESTIONS, WORTHY DREAMS

One of our most articulate teachers is Dr. Sharon Daloz Parks. Her book is entitled *Big Questions, Worthy Dreams*, four words you might substitute every time you read the words sacred purpose. Can we ask *big enough* questions about our identity, community, the intentions of God for the world, and the unfolding of our life over the years we are given? Can we listen to find *worthy dreams* for our lives as we discern our sacred purpose? That's what I wanted for my life—then and now—questions and dreams big enough to send me on a journey to make sense of the complexity of my many worlds, including family of origin, and social, political, and ecclesial cultures.

Can you envision dreams worthy of the identity you have been given as it has been formed, transformed, and even *re-formed* over time? I want to answer Sharon that I have *big questions* that have brought me to choices made in my story and I have been given *worthy dreams* as I learn to listen and read what God is writing in my story. And I want to answer Abba that I understand that how I respond to questions and worthy dreams is not only where my personality, preferences, and passions have led, but *how* I have learned to live in fidelity with what God is writing. "Vocation arises from a deepening understanding of the suffering and wonder of both self and world—and a sense that who you are is in sync with your place in the scheme of things, your "calling," your niche in the ecology of life."[1] "Vocation does not come from willfulness. It comes from listening. I must listen to my life and try to understand what it is truly about—quite apart from what I would like it to be about—or my life will never represent anything real in the world, no matter how earnest my intentions . . . Vocation is not a goal that I pursue. It is a calling that I hear."[2]

We are listening to *someone* who calls. Calling takes place in companionship with God's Spirit, who does the real work. Look at the apparent simplicity of it. Jesus invites us into relationship. The Holy Spirit calls us to live in this relationship in an obedient response to a summons from God. Just because God calls does not mean we always say yes. God starts. Then it is our turn. God responds. Then it is our turn again. What we can count on is basically one sure thing: we are not alone. In a magnificent way, we are in on it. God is writing. We are not passive readers but partners in the work. "If they did anything under their own power at all, it was simply that

---

1. Parks, *Big Questions, Worthy Dreams*, 192.
2. Palmer, *Let Your Life Speak*, 20.

they allowed themselves to fall in love. Jesus showed up, they took one look at each other, and the rest was history. God acted, and the disciples let their nets wash out to sea."[3]

You may not know the name Abraham Joshua Heschel. Born in Poland, educated in 1930s Germany, Heschel was a rabbi and theologian with a heart and mind for both spirituality and activism. He wrote: "Our goal should be to live life in radical amazement . . . [to] get up in the morning and look at the world in a way that takes nothing for granted. Everything is phenomenal; everything is incredible; never treat life casually. To be spiritual is to be amazed."[4] These were inspiring words that he lived as an activist for civil rights and in friendship with Dr. Martin Luther King Jr., whose "I Have a Dream" speech was followed by Heschel's own speech in Washington, DC. Heschel was there at Selma when the troopers beat down peaceful protestors and his voice was heard globally as a call to sacred purpose in relationship with Yahweh and in practical love for others. Social consciousness, for him, was not theoretical, abstract, or an occasional commitment. He told reporters that his feet did the talking that day on the Pettis Bridge in Selma. Like Jesus, Heschel understood that God seeks acts of love as our primary means of giving glory to God. A brilliant theologian, he didn't separate the intersection of knowing God and living to give glory to God through engaged acts of courageous love. Spirituality at its very core is living with sacred purpose to the glory of God for the sake of others. Worship and prayer are a means to something bigger than one individual. Spirituality is expressed in respectful, practical forms of compassion for all.

WORDS WE MAY NOT WANT TO HEAR

Jesus' spirituality says your life isn't exclusively about you, your time isn't only about you, your life has an intentionality *for the sake of others*. The memorable image comes from Frederick Buechner: "The place God calls you is where your deep gladness and the world's deep hunger meet."[5] Finding your voice to speak into the great needs of our time in history, however, is not a call to a soloist. It is a call to join an orchestra. Popular writings about vocation usually point to one's own gifts or passions as the starting place. There is another axis point: "the world's deep hunger," an intersection

3. Taylor, *Home by Another Way*, 40.
4. Heschel, *God in Search of Man*, 46.
5. Buechner, *Wishful Thinking*, 95.

that moves us back to Scripture and into the world. Perhaps we could adapt Buechner's epic quote this way: The place God calls you is where your deep gladness and the world's deep hunger *meet God's inventive intentions for your sacred purpose.* We settle for too little when we decide *our gladness* is enough. To say that you don't need to be aware of the world's deep hunger is a denial of our sacred purpose: our gifts are not given for our benefit but to follow Jesus as he forms the world in his image.

Our lives as the body of Christ are not as independent contractors, each free to do whatever we choose for our self-aggrandizement. There is a point of reference: *God has intentions for the world.* Sacred purpose is to be practiced within a commitment to God's vision for the world; we are not autonomous beings. God is serious in God's intentions and priorities for humankind. The response to God's good gifts is praise, gratitude, and fidelity to God's intentions. And here's a startling thing to ponder: your life is not given to you without strings. Those strings connect you to the world's deep hunger where your identity is rooted in something larger than you alone, God's serious intentions for the world. I need to be honest: it will cost you something as you reimagine your life according to this way of life. It might shake up your assumptions as you read with your questions of heart and mind before you. You may feel as disrupted as Jesus' earliest followers. The other option is to let others tell you what to think, but I'm pretty sure you're reading this book because you're no longer satisfied with being spoon-fed someone else's thoughts.

The starting place in a biblical understanding of spirituality is to discover what God is doing in time and space. Some will scoff at those words, as if God simply left the world in our hands. The Adversary, Satan, thought the same as he tried to convince Jesus as he tested Jesus in the wilderness. Three times he confronted him with alternatives to a God-involved world. To all three tests, Jesus stayed the course of his convictions: "One lives by the Word of God, one does not test the Lord, God alone is to be worshipped." Essentially what he said is the ancient declaration of Israel, *the Shema*, a prayer repeated daily: "The Lord is our God, the Lord alone. You shall love the Lord your God with all your soul and with all you might . . ."(Deuteronomy 6:5). Each challenge from the Adversary was an assault on biblically practiced faith. Jesus was confronted as we are with questions of agenda, authority, and purpose. He faced questions that remains ours, as well: Whose agenda will I serve? Under whose authority will I live? For what purpose am I here? For God alone. *Soli deo gloria.*

Wait, What Did You Say, Lord? I Had Other Plans

PUTTING THE WORLD TO RIGHT

Reading the Bible has been called "thinking God's thoughts after God." Shalom was shattered by sinful disobedience that led to judgment. But God has always had an intention to redeem and restore the earth to shalom and wholeness. I don't know when it finally sunk in for me—the Bible is revelation, a word *from* God, from God's point of view. Read what Moses was called to do in Egypt. Study the prophets who called for covenant faithfulness. "Listen, so that you may live. I will make with you an everlasting covenant . . .Thus says the Lord: Maintain justice and do what is right, for soon my salvation shall come, and my deliverance will be revealed" (Isaiah 55:3, Isaiah 56:1). God will set things right. And we will become menders of our broken world, weavers of new coverings and grace, and visionaries of hope. God calls. God sends. God is actively at work on behalf of the entire cosmos, the universe. God's mission is not only the church, but the world. God will set things right. God will restore shalom (wholeness, peace, harmony) and we are invited to play a role. The outcome is up to God.

Being loved by Abba Father is not only God's gracious gift to you or me *but through us*, to the world. In this era of political and social divisiveness, punitive politics, and vitriolic, disrespectful rhetoric, it has almost become an Old Testament moment for the prophets of God to speak to those who claim to be followers of Jesus and say what Leviticus 19:18 says, "You shall not take vengeance or bear a grudge against any of your people, but you shall love your neighbor as yourself: I am the Lord." As long as Christians build walls of division *against* others, we deny the very pulsing center of our faith. As long as Christians enter the public square armed as "enemies" against those with whom we disagree, we diminish our identity as God's beloved and "make peace with evil" and with our own sense of self-importance and self-absorption.

Our identity as the beloved of God intends to transform selfish egos into tolerance, love, faith, and hope. Instead, we see it distorted into prejudice, bigotry, hatred, and actions that splinter our families, churches, and nation. "Always treat others as you would like them to treat you" (Matthew 7:12). Have we traded in the simplest and most radical form of discipleship for a crushing form of vindictiveness, denigration of others, intolerance, and petty rage? Disrespect has become viral. Our words and ways of communicating are a window into the spiritual condition of our inner selves. The love of Christ is our most powerful evidence of authentic faith in our rabbi only as it is practiced in love of neighbor, "the other," and even our enemies. Arrogance, pride, and egotism is evidence of anything but authentic faith. Jesus told us our identity: we are salt, meant to preserve and heal; we are light meant to shine truth for all to see. "Let your light shine before others, that they may see your good deeds and glorify your Father in heaven" (Matthew 5:16, NIV).

When was the last time you saw Jesus in the face of those with whom you vigorously disagree? I saw the bumper sticker emblazoned on a pickup truck window. Probably sixteen inches in height. "F---" and then the name of a politician. On the bumper was a cross—maybe three inches tall. So, I ask: To what is this man testifying? To whom? What does he teach his children, co-workers, or his neighborhood every time he drives? An important word for our discourse in all of our interactions is *nuance* (shades of meaning or disciplined conversation). Sarcasm, cynicism, vulgarity, and unrefined accusations become highly charged; we lose restraint, respect, and decorum. Disagreement is not the issue; we can disagree, debate, and argue strongly with each other, but it has become uncertain if our entire culture will lose its ability for respectful discourse especially in contested issues.

"Children learn what they live." Our children watch. Our children listen. Our children understand more than we might believe. As followers of Jesus, Christians have a choice to make: *to conform to the culture* that is loud, discordant, harsh, and frequently violent in its words and implications *or to "be transformed by the renewing of your minds*, so that you may discern what is the will of God—what is good and acceptable and perfect" (Romans 12:2, emphasis mine). But the apostle had more to add: "Bless those who persecute you; bless and do not curse them . . . Live in harmony with one another; do not be haughty . . . Do not repay anyone evil for evil but take thought for what is noble on the sight of all. If it is possible, so far as it depends on you, live peaceably with all . . . Do not be overcome by evil, but overcome evil with good" (Romans 12:14, 17, 18, 21).

The spirituality Jesus teaches is one of healing, redemption, and grace within a call for love and unity, not a weaponization of our opinions *against* the other. This is why we need to consistently study the Gospels to watch Jesus show us how to pay attention to Abba and how to know his voice. At the end of the day, following Jesus has become a radically different practice than much of what organized Christianity seems to care about. Following Jesus asks us to transform our culture, not join any movements that are based in violent rhetoric or action. White nationalism is not the way of Jesus, who did not come to bring a violent revolution against Roman occupation or Jewish kings for that matter. Jesus' way was a pathway of inclusion and compassion, not exclusion and animosity. Truth-telling, yes, but speaking truth in love, not violence. Peacemaking? Always.

Jesus knew his sacred purpose. He wasn't confused or uncertain about care for "the least of these" in our communities or about his identity as one sent from the Father as God in human flesh on the sacred ground of the earth. He didn't hesitate to teach us to sit at table with "sinners" of all kinds, including the most religious sinners of the day. He didn't hesitate to sit at table with the marginalized who were not welcomed at the religious tables of the day. He didn't hesitate to break the "rules" of first-century rabbis as he spoke to women (the Samaritan woman), taught theology to women (Mary and Martha), touched the unclean (lepers, the demon-possessed). He didn't hesitate to teach a daily practice of humility or to envision a day when a larger table was set to include people from every tribe, ethnicity, and nation. He and his followers willingly stood in the arena against hypocrisy, religious exclusivism, closed doors, racial superiority, materialism, bigotry, and violence.

If we take Jesus' practices seriously, there is a cost. This commitment can indeed be demanding, as it calls for a radical shift in perspective and behavior. "You shall love the Lord your God with all your heart and with all your soul and with all your mind and with all your strength . . . You shall love your neighbor as yourself" (Matthew 22:37–39). In our identity as the beloved of God, we find our vocation: to love God with all we are—heart, soul, mind, and strength. Your sacred purpose is also to love your neighbor. And that's a problem if you see your neighbor as someone "on the other side of the aisle," or just "other." That's a problem if you live in fear of someone who is different so you not only shun them, reject them, and shut your doors to them even as you build walls *against* them. You keep them out rather than welcome them to the table of your life.

Wendell Berry wrote what may be a catechism of his faith: "I believe that the world was created and approved by love, that it subsists, coheres, and endures by love, and that, insofar as it is redeemable, it can be redeemed only by love. I believe that divine love, incarnate and indwelling in the world, summons the world always toward wholeness that ultimately is reconciliation and atonement with God . . ."[6] Similarly, in Julie Canlis's words, "Our job is not to be extraordinary but to receive the extraordinary blessing that the incarnation brings. Christ's work was then and is now

---

6. Berry, "Health Is Membership."

the same: to sanctify this ordinary life and make it a place of communion again."[7] The purpose of covenant is to restore, reconcile, and redeem people to relationship with God through the atonement of Jesus. As sin separates us from God, salvation restores us to relationship. An ancient Hebrew phrase, *Tikkum Olam*, describes our role in this work. Translated literally it means "repairing of the world" and includes various forms of action that will both repair and improve the world.

THE ARISTIDES PRIORITY

The Roman Emperor Hadrian (117–138) was on the hunt for reasons to outlaw the newly formed Christian religion. He asked one of his officials to gather information that could allow him to crush this new religion. Aristides gives one of the clearest visions for what some might call "true biblical spirituality." To Hadrian's surprise, his report was an honest narrative of what he saw embodied in the Christian community. Instead of an invective against Christians, it became an apologetic for a community practicing their faith in Jesus. Writing in 125, Aristides described his findings about the Christian community but spoke words of affirmation rather than condemnation. As such the document is a snapshot of a community living in fidelity to what they knew of God's intentions. It could well be a manifesto for Jesus' followers in our culture today.

- "They walk in all humility and kindness, and falsehood is not found among them, and they love one another."
- "They despise not the widow, and grieve not the orphan."
- "They distribute liberally and freely to those who are without."
- "If they see a stranger, they bring him under their roof, and rejoice over him, as if he were their own brother."
- "They call themselves brethren, not after the flesh, but after the spirit and in God; but when one of their poor passes away from the world, and any of them see him, then he provides for his burial according to his ability."
- "If they hear that any of their number is imprisoned or oppressed for the name of their Messiah, all of them provide for his needs, and if it is possible that he may be delivered, they deliver him."

7. Canlis, "Incarnation is the Rule."

- "If there is among them a man that is poor and needy, and they have not an abundance of necessaries, they fast two or three days that they may supply the needy with their necessary food."
- "This is really a new kind of person. There is something divine in them."[8]

---

8. A summary of Aristides, *Apology of Aristedes on Behalf of Christians*.

4

What If the Song Has It Wrong? What If This World Is My Home?

You may have heard it said that only certain people do work that is holy. I want to change that to say each of us is called to sacred purpose in all parts of our lives, therefore, everyone has an altar in the world.

"Incarnation means that all ground is holy ground because God not only made it but walked on it, ate and slept and worked and died on it. If we are saved anywhere, we are saved here."
—Frederick Buechner

THE *OIKOS* PRINCIPLE: WHERE IS YOUR ALTAR IN THE HOUSEHOLD OF GOD?

Oikos is a Greek word for household. From *oikos* we also get ecology (*oikologia*) and economy (*oikonomia*). What is the household of God? It's another way to ask, "What matters to God?" Psalm 24:1 gives our answer: "The earth is the Lord's and the fullness thereof." Where is God's household? It is the earth and the fullness thereof; it is creation, *all* of it. God's *oikos*

What If the Song Has It Wrong? What If This World Is My Home?

resides in time and space, temporality and geography, story and context. Spirituality is not detached from here and now. Jesus said "the kingdom has come near" (Mark 1:15). It is accessible to all because the kingdom exists where you are. It is in the details of your story that God speaks, always into the life of you and me as people who lived in a particular time and place like Sarai, Amos, Esther, Ezra, and Ananias. *Oikos* tells us clearly: there is only one household, our earth, and one human family, all of us who live not only *on* the earth but *in* the household of God. Biblical spirituality is grounded in *place*: a household, neighborhood, congregation, and workplace. Incarnation is to the New Testament what *oikos* was to the Hebrew. *Oikos* is the stage of your everyday world. Paul said, "For in him all things were created, things in heaven and earth" (Colossians 1:16).

Oikos is an ancient theological statement: every place is holy ground. The very ground on which we live and move and have our being is the household of God, thus it is holy ground. Spirituality finds meaning in the totality of our story . . . God cares about *all* of life, all of the earth, and yes, all *on* the earth. *Oikos* is a dramatic declaration of God's interest in all of the earth. Read it again: every place is holy ground. That's why we have multiple altars in the world—an altar is a place to honor, serve, and worship God in places we know, live, work, play, and worship.

Most of us skim rapidly past a sentence like the last one because it sounds simplistic: the world is important to God. In a fine and thoughtful video, *Godspeed*, we are introduced to the idea of paying attention to our home as we walk at the speed of holiness,[1] which has been called the slowest of all speeds. We walk at God's pace on the earth to see where God has already been at work, but more, to see where God is at work now. Did it occur to you this morning that your commute might be a place for spiritual nurture, whether you drive, ride, or walk? Did you start the day with an awareness that "today" might be filled with spiritual significance as you pay attention to the presence of God in the very familiar, ordinary steps you take today? Take half an hour to experience *Godspeed*. You may discover extraordinary things that come from living at Godspeed on ordinary days.

In Genesis Yahweh announces that we are given the earth as stewards, not owners. We are caretakers at our many altars in the world. If the earth is God's household, what does that make us, we who inhabit it? The answers are several. We may be guests, but guests were not given dominion over the earth (Leviticus 25:23). We might be "just a passing through." As the old

---

1. Canlis and Canlis, *Godspeed*.

song says, "This world is not my home." But, there's the rub, isn't it? If God's household is the earth, then this world *is* my home. I reside *here*, I serve *here*, I am faithful or not, *here*. We are *not* "just a passing through." We are something else: *we are family*. To no surprise, the word for family in Greek is taken from *oikos*, which means family, or household. In the Psalms we read, "all of you are children of the Highest" (Psalm 82:6, KJV). In 1 John we read, "See what love the Father has given us, that we should be called the children of God; and that is what we are" (3:1).

God's household is the world that we inhabit, it is our home, but there is another "world" where God intends for us to know, the Torah, i.e., the "instructions" of God. No one probably calls it "the instruction manual," but through disciplined reading and historical imagination, we discover the *oikos* of God encompasses both *world* and *word*. Later, Jesus is revealed to us as *logos* in the Greek translated "the word." This is where we find our classroom for vocation: world and word form a symbiotic movement between *relationship* with Abba and *revelation from* Abba. Pay attention to the presence of God in everything (world) as you live awake to seeds of promise embedded in the world (your life), the written word (Torah), and the living Word (Jesus). And don't be surprised when you find yourself given a purpose (calling) and multiple places to serve (your altars in the world).

AN ALTAR IN THE WORLD

Your whole life becomes "an altar in the world"[2] from which to sing your primary opus: *Soli Deo Gloria*. From this starting place comes a lifetime of many iterations of vocation. In religious life, an altar is a sacred place of serving God in worship overseen by ordained clergy. For the rest of us, our altar is a sacred place for serving God in an endless variety of ways and locations. My altar has included numerous tables where I worked: assembly lines at Portable Electric Tools as a high school student, a meat-cutting table in South Saint Paul as a college student, a shipping clerk's table at Deluxe Check Printer's, a library table through four years of theological education, a communion table as a minister of word and sacrament, a pulpit as a parish pastor and campus pastor, a professor's table and lectern at three universities, and a meeting table as the president of The Seattle School of Theology and Psychology.

---

2. See Taylor, *Altar in the World*.

What If the Song Has It Wrong? What If This World Is My Home?

But my altar wasn't limited to work tables, it was in fact found in all the places where I served urban church neighborhoods, including juvenile detention centers, hospital rooms, and people's homes, followed by university dorms, athletic fields, classrooms, counseling rooms, and faculty meeting rooms and a historic graduate school building in Seattle that was built originally as the Chlopek Fishing Company. But even that's not all. Sometimes it was a kitchen table as our family made applesauce, freezer jam, or worked on projects together. Sometimes it was a work bench in a garage, although I am fairly limited in mechanical skills. Sometimes it was a dining room table as we managed the monthly budget, paid bills, or considered a future purchase. Often it was a table over coffee at Bread & Chocolate where we plotted (literally) the next addition to our gardens and imagined a future with the splendor of botanical color for us and our neighbors to enjoy.

If there is a biblical understanding of vocation, this is it. *Our whole life is vocation. Calling is not something we discern once in our lives as we select an occupation: it is our spiritual identity.* Vocation is your spiritual identity: it tells you *who you are* (the beloved of God) and *what you are meant to do* (live to the glory of God). What occupies your time, such as a job or career, is not necessarily the same as your vocation, which is to form a life built around your identity as the beloved of God and shaping your time in faithfulness to the principle of *Soli Deo Gloria*. Can you see the difference? You are called by God to relationship with God—everything from that point forward is about fidelity and obedience.

There's a formational reason for this: Jesus is teaching us how to accept our identity as the beloved and how to love God and one another. That defines how we choose to live. In Genesis 18:19 (NIV) we read an early biblical understanding of the breadth of our spiritual identity: Yahweh says of Abraham, "For I have chosen him, so that he will direct his children and his household after him to keep the way of the Lord by doing what is right and just." Abraham was chosen by God and called to a mission that would change the world, but first it would take root in Abraham and Sarai and through them to their children. It seems to always happen that way: first in the ordinary or local and then it radiates outward to the world. *Who are we? The chosen. What are we meant to do?* Live to the glory of God in our own context and as legacy for the generations that will follow.

In Psalm 116 the poet uses an image of a parent in conversation with a loved child. The translations vary: one says the Lord "inclined his ear," another says "he paid attention to me." *The Living Bible* says "he bends down and listens." I saw Donovan at the coffee shop this week. He's about two and likes trucks. When he saw us, he came running over and pointed to the garbage truck hard at its task. You can guess my instinct: I picked him up and "inclined my ear" to hear his excited chatter about the "big truck." Can you think of Abba God with the tenderness of that image? Right behind Donovan came Juliana, aged eight, filled with enthusiasm, spilling forth joy and just as ready for that hug as Wendy and I are. Abba bends down and listens . . . then inclines toward us to listen and pay attention. Listening is one of our best forms of love.

I offer two snapshots of friends who understand sacred purpose as integral to their spirituality. One left a job as the CEO of a Fortune 500 company because he perceived God's intention for him to mentor young leaders. A scientist, executive corporate leader, not disinterested in his career, but more interested in his calling. I don't believe he's ever looked back. Linda's calling has taken a series of twists and turns, including beating cancer while completing her doctorate. She and her husband, Brian, have a leadership consulting company that transforms how leaders express their brilliance and beauty for the benefit of humanity. Their expertise is in awakening the uniqueness of the individual and their calling as a husband-and-wife duo takes them all over the world, where they live out their individual divine vocations *and* their combined sacred purpose.

These friends know themselves to be people of faith who don't draw a line between work and faith, spirituality and the workplace, discipleship and daily work. It is integral to all of life for them. "Now there are varieties of gifts, but the same Spirit, and there are varieties of service, but the same Lord, and there are varieties of activities but the same God who activates all of them in everyone. To each one is given the manifestation of the Spirit for the common good . . . All these are activated by one and same Spirit, who allots to each one individually just as the Spirit chooses" (1 Corinthians 12:4–7, 11). *Individually. Together.*

> Pause for reflection: Is the concept that you have an altar in the world new to you? If you think of your life as having an altar in the world, what is your primary altar now? What would you describe as your other altars?

What If the Song Has It Wrong? What If This World Is My Home?

SMALL MOMENTS OF TODAY

The surprising thing about biblical spirituality is that God is present in the ordinary, daily, common, and concrete realities of life. Kathleen Norris called one of her books *The Quotidian Mysteries: Laundry, Liturgy and "Women's Work."* Julie Canlis called hers *A Theology of the Ordinary*. Joan Chittister described it as *Wisdom Distilled from the Daily* and Tish Harrison Warren called it *Liturgy of the Ordinary*. Our altar includes the ordinary and daily places we live. Warren is precise: "God is forming us into a new people. And the place of that formation is in the small moments of today."[3] "It is not the heroic nature of our Christian life that is pleasing to God. Nor is it the slim righteousness of obedience to the law. It is . . . communion with God as children of the Father in the everydayness of life . . ."[4] "The whole world has been redeemed and ordinary life with it. Closeness to Christ is found in our ordinary physical existence, not by leaving it behind."[5]

We are called to lifelong purpose: to live in relationship with the Father through the Holy Spirit. Where? In the daily circumstances and environments in which we live. How? By learning to live as apprentices of Jesus' ways and words in our families, work places, neighborhoods, and relationships. It's not magic. The way we live in companionship with Jesus is as learners—practitioners. We learn to listen, to be attentive to what we hear, what we know, and what is being made known to us by the presence of the Spirit moving and speaking within. What will be found as we do? God's presence and God's silence, the beauty of creation, the gracious gift of forgiveness, the drama of mercy, the joy of gratitude, and wisdom for living in ordinary time.

One of the most dramatic teachings of Jesus in the Sermon on the Mount is about quiet and small things: light and salt. In the face of all that is massively wrong in our fractured, divided, violent, and weaponized culture, Jesus called us (our vocation) to be what we already are as followers of Jesus: salt and light—doing our work quietly in a loud world. It sounds like an improbable way to bring transformation but it is Jesus' way. Salt was a preservative in the first century; spiritually it is a means to preserve the kingdom of God against inhumanity, oppression, and wounds. Light is our vocation to live brightly in the darkness so that we bring glory to God.

---

3. Warren, *Liturgy of the Ordinary*, 21.
4. Canlis, *Theology of the Ordinary*, 34.
5. Canlis, *Theology of the Ordinary*, 45.

As we follow Jesus we shine our lives on his words and his ways. These are audacious words to fishermen, tax collectors and zealots-turned-disciples, prostitutes, and broken people who had only lived in the darkness of demons, disease, broken bodies, blindness, incarceration, and pain. As you find your sacred purpose, you are part of a scandalous plan to preserve, brighten, and shine in our darkened culture.

WHAT I LEARNED FROM THE PIZZA GIRL

At our local pizza place, I stood outside waiting to leave. I asked a young worker standing with a rake. "What else do you out here, besides smile and rake the gravel around the picnic tables?" She answered, "Well, this is kind of a dead time, but usually I serve this area." I asked her name. I didn't expect to hear God's voice so clearly in the timbre of a high school girl. "My name is Angel Rose." She wasn't finished. "Angel means a messenger from God and Rose refers to signature of God. That's who I am. A messenger of God signed by God. My mother said the messenger of God came to her and gave her the name." Angel Rose understood: Our identity is given. Such a deep knowledge at age seventeen. "A messenger of God signed by God." She knows her identity in convictional clarity. Angel Rose said she tries to live her identity in her work and relationships. Perhaps we should listen attentively next time we get a pepperoni pizza!

ETERNITY DWELLING IN TIME AND SPACE

Jesus walked in companionship with real people in real communities in real time and a real place. But there's more to it than the historic. Jesus *continues* to walk with us and invites us into companionship in the most ordinary, commonplace, daily moments. God doesn't disdain creation. "The One who inhabits eternity comes to dwell in time."[6] In Jesus God moves into the ordinary, mundane, and human places you and I live in. What that means for jobs, work, and careers cannot be overstated: *All work is God's work.* From major leadership positions to what are seen as minor and unimportant roles, all work is God's work. We can thus accurately speak of *occupational calling—calling to a job*. Out of our vocation (a living relationship with Jesus) we listen to our story for our calling, including our jobs. This is

---

6. Buechner, *Now and Then*, 61.

What If the Song Has It Wrong? What If This World Is My Home?

not to discount or diminish the important opportunity our jobs provide us to bring glory to God.

I worked for many years in campus ministry—I was a professor but also a pastor on college campuses. In those settings I was responsible to plan and lead chapel services for students, faculty, and staff. I asked Kirk, one of our art profs, to throw a pot while I talked about creation in one of those chapels. I was at the lectern with a light to illuminate my notes and Kirk was off to one side with a potter's wheel and a spotlight on him. He started as I began to speak. He prepared the clay, started spinning the wheel, and did what an excellent potter does—he used his skill to create. That was my point in my chapel words. But the words were not the focus—the pot he created was. It started as a lump of clay, literally and symbolically, and emerged as a large vase. I couldn't see his work but I could hear the murmurs, oohs and aahs of the students. Then, there came an audible gasp as he collapsed what had become an already beautiful vase. He collapsed it and started again. The audience was aghast. And then, with the skill of his craft, he crafted a new version from the same lump of clay. The work of his hands matched the work of my words as I spoke of God as an artist with mind, skill, and heart as he forms us in his own image and likeness. That day, hundreds of students saw that we live our lives in the hands of a potter-artist, starting out with us as an unformed lump of clay but willing for us to be collapsed and then to start over again in a process of transformation to usefulness and beauty. We live in the hands of a potter-artist of utmost skill, able to create, transform, and redeem.

Take a moment to think about someone you know who lives with single-minded purpose. Do you wonder how they came to live with such a deep spirituality? I love to be around those people because they know themselves to be loved and remind themselves of their core convictions. They make daily choices to live courageously into their sacred purpose. I know a woman who works in the area of sexual trauma and abuse. She works every day knowing she will hear stories from victims and perpetrators alike that could brutalize her spirit, enrage her sensitivities, and damage her soul . . . unless. She starts every day in prayer for herself, her protection and well-being. She knows she is at risk every time she opens her office door, not only to possible physical assault but to the deepest kind of emotional and spiritual assault. So, she does not go into her office until she is prepared, made ready by the Holy Spirit, reminded of God's ferocious love for her. Only when she knows herself to be ready to face the spiritual warfare of her office, will she leave home to practice her calling. Her altar is a place surrounded by darkness, potential violence, and emotional trauma. She has served God faithfully in what she knows herself to be called. She is an icon of spiritual courage.

At the core of biblical teachings on worship is the essential practice of Sabbath. Regularly, the Sabbath rhythm calls us to stop our busy activity for a crucial sacred purpose: to gratefully acknowledge the rule of Yahweh. Literally, the word *sabbath* means stop or cease, but there's a second clause: we stop in order to recognize our call to rest physically but also to rest in what God is doing as we are *not* doing.

Vocation isn't always about *what* you do but it is always about *how you do* what you find yourself called to do. Your calling has everything to do with *how* you are as teacher, parent, friend, nurse, manager, tech, banker, pharmacist, custodian, artist, or writer. Following Jesus is always about *how* you do whatever you are called to do. You are called to participate in something good God intends for you that the world needs. We call this sacred purpose. Live *Soli Deo Gloria*. Do all to the glory of God knowing you live in the presence of God. Worship is one of the most important ways we live *Soli Deo Gloria*. "If the incarnation made ordinary life holy, then all things in life can and *must* be brought to worship."[7]

Standing just above the Western Wall in Jerusalem, known to many as "the Wailing Wall," I joined a growing crowd of Jerusalemites and tourists, gathering to march down the hill singing, "Make a joyful noise to the Lord, all the earth. Serve the lord with gladness; come into his presence with singing." (Psalm 100:1–2). I had no preparation for what was to follow. In one of the most remarkable moments of worship in my life, I felt the urge to sing, dance, and celebrate. I *felt* it. I didn't think it. It was natural in that moment to make noise joyfully. We reached the broad esplanade and formed a circle dance of as many as a hundred people. I knew the students with whom I traveled. The rest were not known to me, but I cannot use the word "stranger" to describe any of them. In that moment of noisy joy, we were anything but strangers. We became a congregation of boisterous friends celebrating Yahweh enthusiastically with the words of Scripture. Perhaps we should try that in Protestant worship—march to the street in front of the altar and sing, dance, shout, and glorify God.

---

7. Canlis, *Theology of the Ordinary*, 44.

5

Get Used to Different; We Call It the Kingdom of God

You may have heard it said that your life is yours to live, plan, and create. I want to change that and say get used to different; we start with God's priorities on our way to sacred purpose.

It shouldn't surprise us that God has priorities and intentions for the world and your life purpose.

THE JUSTICE PRIORITY

Justice is not an afterthought to the God of Scripture. Not everyone believes that anymore. For some it is seen merely as the agenda of "the other side." That's a problem: Scripture shows us that God prioritizes justice almost page by page. To say otherwise is to mute what God has written all through the story of covenant people. Some today say Jesus' teachings are passé and "weak." That too is a problem. You'll have to decide: Do you intend to follow Jesus in the way of Jesus or someone else? Are biblical priorities for just one nation, party, or viewpoint? The God who shows no favoritism insists on a compassionate and redemptive reading of Scripture. Read carefully and see if you agree: there doesn't seem to be a spirit of "in or out," "us or them," "we or they." There is one family to which we all belong.

- "Yahweh executes justice for the fatherless and the widow" (Deuteronomy 24:17).
- "You shall also love the stranger, for you were strangers in the land of Egypt" (Deuteronomy 10:18).
- "You shall not follow a majority in wrongdoing . . . you shall not side with the majority so as to pervert justice; not shall you be partial to the poor in a lawsuit . . . You shall not oppress a resident alien . . ." (Exodus 23:1–3, 9).
- "Learn to do good; seek justice, rescue the oppressed, defend the orphan, plead for the widow" (Isaiah 1:17).
- "But seek the welfare of the city . . . and pray to the Lord on its behalf, for in its welfare, you will your welfare" (Jeremiah 29:7).

The Talmud recorded debates between rabbis in the second through fifth century AD. The justice theme was not up for debate. "Do not be daunted by the enormity of the world's grief. Do justice . . . now. Love mercy . . . now. Walk humbly . . . now. You are not obligated to complete the work but neither are you free to abandon it."[1] Rabbi Toba Spitzer is clear in his view of the Jewish value of justice: "In Jewish thought, justice isn't merely about how things work, but how they ought to be."[2] I cannot escape the insistence of these words: God has a tender heart for those who are vulnerable, alone, weak, oppressed, and the outsiders, all those who feel their backs against the wall. You can try to evade this but you have to willfully stifle the thunder of God's love for such people. There are movements today that claim a Christian agenda but unless that agenda includes biblical justice, it is like a noisy gong or a clanging cymbal. Our time in history is not a time to disengage but rather to embrace the world in compassion, seeking justice for all. And that is the precise focus of what some call "God's bias" toward the vulnerable. Ultimately it is God's way of creating a just society for all where equity is the intention of YHWH. "The justice that is proposed and for which concrete implementation is provided, moreover, is a social practice in which the maintenance, dignity, security, and well-being

---

1. Shapiro, *Pirke Avot*, 2:16.
2. Spitzer, *Tzedek*, 1.

Get Used to Different; We Call It the Kingdom of God

of every member of the community are guarded in concrete ways."[3] "For the word of the Lord is upright, and all his work is done in faithfulness. He loves righteousness and justice; the earth is full of the steadfast love of the Lord" (Psalm 33:5). This is *how* God created, *why* God ordered creation to operate in this specific ethical lifestyle, and *what* God's serious intentions are for all who live in faithfulness to God's sacred intentions for all.

Returning to Scripture, we remember that Jesus was born a Jew in first-century Palestine. He and his parents were refugees in Egypt as they escaped political persecution from the Jewish king. Jesus was a poor Jew. When Mary brought gifts to the altar in fulfillment of Levitical law, she brought inexpensive turtledoves, not a lamb. Remember, Jesus was in the underclass in the Roman empire, living under oppression with Roman presence on every corner. Injustice and poverty were an existential experience for his community. His understanding of God's priorities moved him to act. Jesus was handed the scroll from the elders in the synagogue to read from Isaiah.

> The Spirit of the Lord is upon me, because he has anointed me to bring good news to the poor. He has sent me to proclaim release to the captives and recovery of sight to the blind, to let the oppressed go free, to proclaim the year of the Lord's favor. (Luke 4:19–20)

The drama begins: He was deliberate and careful as he rolled up the scroll to return it to the holy ark that houses the Torah (Luke 4:20). The drama builds. What came from his mouth were words they did not expect to hear, words that scandalized his community. "Today this Scripture has been fulfilled in your hearing" (Luke 4:21). It started well but when the implications registered, his listeners were filled with rage. Why? Jesus declared himself the fulfillment of this messianic text, naming himself as the one sent to preach, proclaim, give sight, free, and proclaim Jubilee to all. The local boy named himself the one called by God to return first-century Jews to the heart of God. Jesus defined his own calling in a messianic mandate of justice advocacy. He calls us to do the same. If we follow Jesus, it's not an option; it is part of our sacred purpose. Compassion will always prompt us to live aware of those in need, but more, to both advocate and support.

The poor are not only those who face social, economic, and political oppression but those who, with humility, seek the Lord. "Those who tremble at the word of God" (Isaiah 66:5). Proclamation is needed: we declare a

---

3. Brueggemann, *Theology of the Old Testament*, 189.

way to change hearts so Jesus defines his mission as preaching good news. Justice advocacy is likewise essential for the refugees of Isaiah's day and those bound in Jesus' day and ours. And compassionate action is found in giving sight, freedom, and justice. And: "The greatest of these is love" (1 Corinthians 13:13). "Those who show *compassion,* in whatever form, realize that without a message that changes hearts and without a just society, their work is incomplete."[4]

My experience was different. I was part of a white church in the 1960s that saw our "sister church" in our denomination caught up in the riots after the murder of Martin Luther King Jr. I saw the smoke on the South and West Sides of the city as I took the train downtown. Did our congregation come to the assistance of that church? We did not. Did we teach the themes listed above and work for caring and compassionate engagement with others? We did not. We chose the sidelines, not the arena. We were a privileged white suburban congregation. We were unable to see the needs just twenty-five miles removed from our suburban homes. But history has taught us to wake up, have ears to hear, and care deeply about what moves the heart of God.

What opened my eyes occurred when I found myself in an inner-city church in St. Paul as a college student. Scarcity was the norm in our working-class poor white neighborhood. I watched paychecks poured out at local taverns. I saw Jimmy, age ten, wandering the streets at 1:00 AM because he was afraid to be home alone while his parents drank up their weekly paycheck. I could no longer *not* see what I knew of families living on the margins.

What woke me up further was my relationship with an African American pastor in the poorest neighborhood in my city, Dr. Earnest Brazill. Part of a group of pastors, we met monthly for "Black-White Clergy Dialogue," where I learned face-to-face and heart-to-heart through honest and sometimes painful discourse. I began to understand what my white upper-middle-class background never let me see—obvious and unconscious bias, white privilege, and absent biblical truths. I grew up in a church that taught us salvation but not justice, evangelism but not God's concern for the poor, the widows, orphans, and strangers in the land (immigrants?).

Three words described my experience. They might be a protocol to move us forward on this contentious subject of racial justice in American culture: *dialogue, relationality, honesty.* Even the name of our gatherings told a story, "Black-White Clergy Dialogue." We were African American

---

4. Bailey, *Jesus Through Middle Eastern Eyes,* 162.

Get Used to Different; We Call It the Kingdom of God

and Caucasian. These were times of discourse. We met face-to-face, relationally. We literally had to *see* each other. Curt Thompson makes a moving observation: "we were born looking for someone who is looking for us."[5] All of us long to be recognized, seen, and respectfully and lovingly welcomed. Professor Itihari Y. Touré says, "The South African ritual of greeting, 'Sawubona,' . . . means . . . *I see you, I see your spiritual essence and all those in your lineage who carry this same essence.*"[6] In our gatherings, we were people meeting to learn from each other. And we did so with some level of honesty. I understand why that part might be hard—we can feel criticized, scolded, or typecast by another, we assume we'll be judged and labeled or that we'll say the wrong thing and create new enmity. But if we are followers of Jesus, we are not free to turn away our face from each other.

Bono said: "But the one thing we can all agree—all faiths, all ideologies—is that God is with the vulnerable and poor. God is in the slums, in the cardboard boxes where the poor play house. God is in the silence of a mother who has infected her child with a virus that will end both their lives. God is in the cries heard under the rubble of war. God is in the debris of wasted opportunity and lives, and God is with us if we are with them."[7] Bono is hard to ignore: "It's annoying, but justice and equality are mates. Aren't they? Justice always wants to hang out with equality. And equality is a real pain."[8] The church must do more than sing sentimentally about righteousness, reconciliation, and peace.

What happens if we are no longer awake to God's priority for justice? It's not hard to answer: it changes our value of people. We no longer see others as created in the image of God. Howard Thurman, a theologian at Boston University, was subjected to injustice as a young African American raised in the south. In his analysis of the roots of injustice and racial hatred, he said "there is *contact between people without fellowship,* i.e., relationships become transactions rather than *koinonia*; forget the second great command: to love neighbor as thyself."[9]

---

5. Thompson, *Soul of Shame*, 138.
6. Touré, *Ritual is a Means of Remembering the Human Spirit*, 1.
7. Nigro, ed., *Spirituality of Bono*.
8. Bono, US National Prayer Breakfast, 2006.
9. Thurman, *Jesus and the Disinherited*, 75.

On Holy Ground

THE COVENANT PRIORITY: WE BELONG TO GOD; WE TRUST IN GOD

There's a covering, a sacred canopy that has authority over my life, and gives meaning to it. Biblical writers called it *covenant*, fidelity. Words that will not let me evade what it means, membership in an imperfect human community. Covenant for Israel was a promise God made to them and an often failed promise they made to Yahweh. God would always be their God; they promised to obey. They called it "cutting" a covenant (Genesis 15:9–10). Sadly for us, our covenants have become transactions, our priest's, attorneys, and our agreements, financial. "The primary propensity of Israel is to focus on Yahweh's fidelity, expressed particularly in the terms *merciful, gracious, abounding in steadfast love, and faithfulness* . . . Israel's most elemental and most recurring practice is to speak about Yahweh's reliability and trustworthiness."[10]

In my life, I entered into covenant with Jesus as a ten-year-old in my baptism. I didn't know much of what I was getting into but I longed that every word they spoke over me could be true. I was baptized in the name of the Father, the Son, and the Holy Spirit, marked by the cross of Christ by the Spirit forever. I now belong to God. Marked by this baptism, God does not give up on me, even if I give up on myself. Read again: God does not give up on me, even if I give up on myself.

In my wedding in 1970, I made another covenant in the name of Jesus when I married Wendy Lee McJunkin. I cannot erase that reality. It marks me in ways that brings grace and delight and scars and sadness and the deepest possible fulfillment. In my ordination in the fall of 1975, I made yet another covenant. I took the vows of ordination as an American Baptist clergy. I cannot erase that reality. I no longer function as a minister in a local parish but I am *always* ordained.

I know my failings in both marriage and ministry. But in each case, something happened. It was not a contract but a covenant that I just can't shake—in covenant, we declare our intention to fidelity. I entered covenants at ten, twenty-one, and twenty-six. The one with whom I entered covenant has not failed me. Yes, God has confused me, troubled me, and caused me sleepless nights, but told me in covenant, "I will never leave you or forsake you" (Deuteronomy 31:8). I wish I felt it in a visceral way every day and in the dark nights of the soul. I may not always feel it, but somewhere deep

---

10. Brueggemann, *Theology of the Old Testament*, 226.

inside I know it to be the truest thing there is in this universe. In covenant, we find over and over: we belong to God just as God belongs to us as our loving Abba Father. And this must be said: The God to whom we belong is always the God to be obeyed. "Observe what I command you today" (Exodus 34:11). Yahweh is a God who commands and the response of God's people is obedience. Obediently we resonate with the intentions of this One who loves us. Just as in any human relationship of love, we see, hear, and, love in return; the one who calls us does so out of irrepressible love.

THE PRIORITY OF THE TABLE

Jesus spent a great deal of time with people at meals. He invited unexpected people to eat with him, including a tax collector, prostitutes, a revolutionary, and other known "sinners." He invited the "poor, crippled, lame and blind" so they would all be blessed. Speaking metaphorically, *table* means we don't come to faith alone, and we don't continue in faith without the companionship of table in its many forms. Table spirituality is eucharistic, a time to break bread and drink the cup of wine, symbolic of Jesus' death and sacrifice. "Eucharist" comes from the Greek word *eucharistia*, which means thanksgiving. The table is essential to the life of the church because it reveals companionship "on the way" *in remembrance of him*. As a pastor my most loved responsibility was to offer bread and cup to a congregation I had come to love deeply. In some traditions, Eucharist is a sacramental way for Christians to participate in Christ's sacrifice and receive grace and salvation. In other traditions, Eucharist is more a symbolic ritual of remembrance, a living memorial of joining with Jesus in an eternal covenant, made possible by the atonement represented in the cup of wine.

> While they were eating, Jesus took bread, said the blessing, broke it, and giving it to his disciples said, "Take and eat; this is my body." Then he took a cup, gave thanks, and gave it to them, saying, "Drink from it, all of you, for this is my blood of the covenant, which will be shed on behalf of many for the forgiveness of sins." (Matthew 26:26–28)

The table is also symbolic for everyday life: we gather to engage friends, mentors, elders, and strangers around tables. At our local coffee shop, we have found friendship and connections. Our table there, is, in fact, a type of altar in our world. We don't sing or pray aloud, but we are intentional to *see* and celebrate people, young and old, baristas and customers. We live in a Navy town with people in uniforms, young families familiar with the absence of a parent on deployment. Today we drove past a house on our street with a big sign: "Welcome back, Daddy. We missed you." The family couldn't wait for Daddy to return to his seat at the table.

"The Word of God is sacramental. That means it is sacred, and as a sacred word, it makes present what it indicates . . . Through his [Jesus'] words, he became really present to them . . . The word creates what it expresses . . . God spoke light and light was . . . When we say that God's word is sacred, we mean that God's word is full of God's presence . . . Our little stories are lifted up into God's great story and there given their unique place . . . Our daily, ordinary lives are, in fact, sacred lives that play a necessary role in the fulfillment of God's promises."[11]

In Ancient Israel, to invite someone to table was a way to welcome them into your tent, to declare solidarity with *the other*. It thus becomes an altar of companionship. It is one of Jesus' most poignant practices and controversial teachings: he crossed racial boundaries, cultural divisions, and economic barriers. He was condemned as a "friend of sinners," but for Jesus this was a sign that his teachings were getting through. Jesus invited everyone to his table, and into "his tent" as his act of radical inclusivity. Are we not called to do the same?

I have not been to war. I have many family members and friends who have. One thing they all share: reticence to talk of their experience. Ron was one of those friends, with three tours in Vietnam as a helicopter gunner. His job was to protect the wounded and he could only do that by wounding and killing "the enemy." At his job, some years later, a conveyor belt accident took off the foot of a worker. As others panicked, he stanched the flow of blood, then gathered scattered pieces of bone and foot and put them in ice for the paramedics who arrived soon after. I met him at the hospital and watched him tell the man's wife her husband would live but the recovery would be long. I went to his home with kielbasa and Coors beer. As we sat at table, the words finally flowed, the stories were told, tears were shed, anger was expressed, and, mercifully, sleep finally overtook him.

I thought I would hear stories of hatred for the enemy, clarity for the mission, and certainty about the war. I did not. What I heard instead was overwhelming sadness at the loss of life—on both sides. What I heard instead was sorrow at the carnage and death deemed necessary enough to declare others to be the enemy. I protested the war and voted for those I

---

11. Nouwen, *With Burning Hearts*, 54, 55, 59.

hoped would bring it to an end. On that Ron and I were in serious disagreement. We had our moments to argue and debate. We disagreed, but we met often in the morning for coffee at one porch or another; we climbed Little Tahoma on Mount Rainier together and he saved me from a fall into a steep crevasse. I conducted his wedding. I baptized his children. When we moved he brought me a parting gift—a medal he received in combat. And we parted as brothers in the faith.

There will be wars until the very end of time. There will be enemies against whom nations will fight. We will disagree in the political arena. We will argue over values in dispute. It's been that way since early in the story of humankind. It is naivete, I am told, to believe it can be otherwise. And yet, I have lived long enough to see enemies become allies, warfare turn into economic partnerships, and enemies become neighbors. In the shadows and fog of rancor, vitriol, fractured relationships, the weaponization of words, and bitter disrespect, I hear the voice of one called the Son of Man who calls us to fight differently with the weapon of love. We can be people of conviction, even strongly opposite convictions, and still be people of discourse, respect, love, and fruitful political engagement.

Jesus lived his life and taught his disciples in a culture of military occupation and political oppression. He pointed to a new kingdom, but not one to be won by warfare. Instead, boldly, fiercely, he made his claim and gave his call: "You have heard that it was said, 'You shall love your neighbor and hate your enemy.' But I say to you, Love your enemies and pray for those who persecute you, so that you may be children of your Father in heaven . . ." (Matthew 5:42–43). Knowing full well who his enemies *should be* (Caesar, Herod, Samaritans, and those who plotted to kill him), he stood in the breach with a consistent message of love. Naïve? Some say it even today. And in those shadows of hatred his voice remains steadfast and clear: Love. Love Abba. Love your neighbor. Love your enemies as reconcilers, peacemakers, and healers in our very broken culture. Can you join his movement? Get used to different.

AND ONE MORE: THE PRIORITY OF INTEGRITY

We can practice integrity at whatever table we perform our daily tasks. Many look for ways to find a shortcut. John Wooden, the iconic basketball coach, said: "The true test of a man's character is what he does when no one is watching."[12] That's not just a good pep talk at a basketball practice, but a viable image of our calling. "Let every detail in your lives ... be done in the name of the Master, Jesus, thanking God the Father every step of the way" (Colossians 3:17, The Message).

My father and his business partner owned a lithographic platemaking shop in Chicago. Late in his life he lamented that he had never been a pastor or missionary and concluded that his life had been a failure. I knew better and told him so. *How* they managed their business was honorable, generous, and full of integrity. They were honest. They had a set of moral guidelines they would not break. They cared for the families of forty-plus employees and provided for their needs. These were men of integrity. They once turned down a lucrative job because they didn't believe God was in it. My father did not teach by words. He taught by *how* he lived every day. His curriculum was significant, his quiet pedagogy was profound.

How we are, *how* we act, *how* we show up at to serve God are good guidelines, don't you think? To be moral, honorable, and, full of integrity? "Work must be good work before it can call itself God's work ... No crooked table legs or ill-fitting drawers ever, I dare swear, came out of the carpenter's shop at Nazareth."[13] Wendell Berry says it gracefully: "Elton loved the use of his mind that revealed the possibilities within places and showed him the work that needed to be done. He loved offering himself to his work. He loved the knowledge of what one man's skill and strength could do in a day. He farmed as a lover loves."[14] What then does it mean to serve God and people to the glory of God as an airline pilot? "Land the plane!"[15] As a doctor? Heal your patients. As waitstaff? Serve the food. Manage the corporation. Balance the books. You fill in the blanks. Do so in a daily practice of integrity.

Paul writes in Philippians 4: "Keep on doing the things you have learned ... from me." He continued:

- Whatever is honorable (venerable, what has been called "nobly serious")
- Whatever is just (fair to all, not to some)
- Whatever is pure (fit for service, authentic)

---

12. Wooden, "True Test."
13. Sayers, *Creed or Chaos*, 56–57.
14. Berry, *Place in Time*, 228.
15. Keller, *Redefining Work*.

Get Used to Different; We Call It the Kingdom of God

- Whatever is commendable (compelling)
- Whatever is excellent (like a first-rate tool needed for a task)
- Whatever is worthy of praise (or has a good name)

To live with integrity is to live true. Place those words where you will see them. It might change how you approach life every day. *Knowing* the way and *going* the way are different. The New Testament word *sincerity* could be a synonym for integrity. To live sincerely is to live literally "without wax." When unethical potters and merchants found a crack or a chip in pottery, they didn't discount the price or start over, they covered the crack with wax to hide the crack, and then covered the crack with a deceiving decorative paint—they were *without integrity*, their lives were, therefore, *insincere*. To be sincere means we no longer cover the cracks within to hide them.

> Pause for reflection: Which priorities in this chapter surprised you? Do you find yourself in sync with any of them in particular? Did any one cause you an urgency for deeper practices?

6

God Comes to You Disguised as Your Life

> *You may have heard it said that vocation/sacred purpose is primarily about keeping a journal of your natural talents and your greatest hopes. I want to change that a bit. Finding your sacred purpose comes as you let your life speak to help you identify your identity in Jesus.*

"Listen to your life. See it for the fathomless mystery it is. In the boredom and pain of it, no less than in the excitement and gladness: touch, taste, smell your way to the holy and hidden heart of it, because in the last analysis all moments are key moments and life itself is grace."[1] Do Buechner's words make sense to you? Pay attention to your story to find your identity? *Listen to your life for the story it is.* Good idea, but how do we do that? Try this: sit up, take note, pay attention, reflect on when and where you sense God's presence, listen for "rumors of angels." And, "become *a detective for divinity*."[2] "Before you tell your life what you intend to do with it, listen for what it intends to do with you. Before you tell your life what

---

1. Buechner, *Now and Then*, 87.
2. Taylor, *Preaching Life*, 15.

truths and values you have decided to live up to, let your life tell you what truths you embody, what values you represent."[3]

We are formed by narrative. Human identity is formed narratively—we are who we are as a result of the stories we tell and retell. Some write our stories in memoirs, autobiographies, and journals, while most of us *tell* our stories orally. It happens *in vivo,* on the way to something else. Increasingly we tell our stories in texts, emails, and social media. Living with sacred purpose involves the ability to read all your story—knowing and speaking what is true about yourself. We remember in part because stories will not let us go. We tell stories to make meaning of our lives. We remember stories of meaning to understand our sacred purpose. Your story is more than a diary of what you already know about yourself: it is a living conversation of curious reflection, as you continue to discover what the Spirit is writing in your unfolding life. It is listening deeply to the Spirit in all parts of your life.

Listening to Jesus' words is one way we know God's heart and mind as we seek our sacred purpose. God is writing my story and directing us all to return to a richly biblical view of vocation, which is a way of reading your story with curiosity and wonder in relationship with God. For some these words sound otherworldly, as if meant for only a special monastic kind of person. Perhaps that's because we have stopped reading Scripture to learn how Jesus intends our faith to be childlike. "Whoever becomes simple and elemental again, like this child, will rank high in God's kingdom" (Matthew 18:35, The Message).

Jesus doesn't soften his words in Matthew 28:18–20, the Great Commission.

- *I have something for you to do*: "Go, therefore and make disciples of all nations, baptizing them, teaching them to observe all things that I have told you." *Purpose.*
- *I have something to say*: "All authority in heaven and on earth has been given to me." *Listening.*
- *I have something to give you*: "I am with you always to the end of the age." *Belonging."*

"Let your life speak" means *look inward*. Sacred purpose is found in your sacred identity. There you will find the fingerprint of God writing "your sacred design." Each element of your self-identity has value. Of

---

3. Palmer, *Let Your Life Speak*, 4.

course, look inward to your dreams. Of course, look inward to your deep visions for your life—those dreams are not to be pushed aside. Pay attention to what matters to you and the capacities that are distinctively yours, but remember the great *before* of God who knew you as God formed you, *before* your birth. Can you hear it? God *precedes* you. Remember the *before of God* who is always ahead of you *before* you ruminate on options and opportunities that appear to "present" themselves. Jesus said, "Your Father knows what you need *before* you ask him" (Matthew 6:8). *Before* is also where God lives, awaiting our arrival. When you identify "sacred design," the pathway may be through your dreams, visions, and opportunities as you read the story *God is* writing in partnership with you. "When I study and understand my life story, I can then join God as coauthor. I don't have to settle for merely being a reader of my life; God calls me to be a *writer of my future*. He asks me to take the only life I will ever be given and shape it in the direction he outlines for me. I am to keep writing, moving forward into the plot that God has woven into the sinews of my soul."[4]

Paula D'Arcy said it evocatively: "God comes to us disguised as our life."[5] As we listen to our life as story, we will find glimpses of our altar in the world; we will no longer be surprised that we have many particular places to live into our calling(s) (where) and the unlimited ways we will be called to do our work (how). Annie Dillard said, "You were made and set here for this, to give voice to your own astonishment."[6] Where it begins is with God who made you and set you in place, this God who penetrates the earth with beauty, glory, and presence, and evokes astonishment, which then gives voice to what we see, hear, sense, and know of God.

READING BIBLICAL NARRATIVE

I am aware the Bible may be a barrier for some because the church has been hurtful to some or even done them wrong. Reading Scripture can sometimes seem complex, requiring many years of academic study. The Bible, however, is primarily a narrative of the stories of ancient people of faith on the same search for meaning, vocation, and belonging as you are. They are not heroes of faith but ordinary women and men on a trek in their own time and in the geography of their context. I don't read about them

---

4. Allender, *To Be Told*, 34.
5. Quoted in Rohr, *Falling Upward*, 151.
6. Dillard, *Writing Life*, 68.

because they alone have wisdom to give but because I trust their narratives to be as human as I am. That means some of them were skeptics who needed to touch the wound of Jesus' side to move forward in faith. Some were deceivers like Jacob the serial swindler. Some were betrayers of Jesus like Judas and Peter. Some were adulterers like David or violent like many across biblical narratives. And, some, like Jesus' mother, Mary, started with words I have struggled to say in my life, "Let it be to me as you have said." We don't have a glimpse into her inner thoughts as a teenaged girl visited by God's messenger, but somehow she heard enough to say *yes, let it be*. All biblical narratives can be read as stories of creation, fall, and redemption.

I read biblical stories because the humanity depicted there is as flawed, failed, and finite as is mine (and yours). I need to read them with a historical imagination to let their words, struggles, prayers, and faith inspire me to my own faith. We are not only looking for historical explanation; we are on the hunt for a way to engage texts and our story. Reading biblical narratives helps us become skilled at reading our own life as story. I imagine faces as I picture each character; I hear the timbre of voices and the joyful sound of laughter. As I read, I pay attention for the sacred voice of Abba in their stories. When we listen for sacred voice in biblical texts, we learn to listen for sacred voice in our own stories. Perhaps that is why I ground my story in biblical texts.

We find ourselves in on a conversation with God about ourselves and the world in which we find ourselves. Let the narratives be as alive to your life as your own story is. I don't exaggerate. Historical imagination is engaged when we read the Bible as *our* story and not merely ancient history. It was the brilliant professor James Muilenberg who said: "Until you can read the story of Adam and Eve, of Abraham and Sarah, of David and Bathsheba, as your own story . . . you have not really understood it."[7] We experience, in human terms *now,* what our ancestors experienced in their lives *then*. This is a biblical form well-known to ancient Judaism that we might call our narrative memory. The *Shema* is one of our most sacred biblical practices.

In Deuteronomy six we are told that God gave texts, statutes, and ordinances for children and future generations (including us) "so that you'll live in deep reverence before God lifelong . . ." (Deuteronomy 6:2, The Message). Israel remembered their suffering in exile but also their rescue in the exodus out of Egypt. Future generations were invited into the narrative memory as members of a community that was not only past but present

---

7. Buechner, *Listening to Your Life*, 36.

and future. Ritualistically, when the children would ask the elders to remember the most important historical event of the Exodus, the elders told them the story of Moses, Exodus, and Passover. Future generations would enter the Exodus through the narrative of memory. Future generations did not experience the Exodus firsthand as their ancestors did; instead, they experienced God's deliverance as they engaged the text firsthand with a keen, creative historical imagination.

And . . . there is more. We can find and share our humanity with what we perceive as *their experience,* but let's be clear. We come to the culture, history, and context of biblical story as outsiders. Reading the text is always an invitation to enter the world and ideology of the writer. An essential question is to ask, "are there vested interests" in the writer, the story and in me as a reader? Early Mosaic texts created a worldview of deliverance *vis a vis* the Exodus while Solomonic texts focus on the order created by monarchy. Jeremiah was a critic of royal practices. I grew up in northern American cities. Although I have been to Israel, I know little of life in the desert or mountains of ancient Palestine. I have never eaten manna, nor have you. I have never lived under the political oppression of an empire who held my people and nation under occupation. Some of you may have. I was raised in a relatively economically comfortable lifestyle but knew scarcity in my early years. I have studied under many professors, some even excellent teachers, but I have not left my life to follow a rabbi as did Peter, James, John, and the rest. I did not grow up in an honor/shame culture where people were considered "clean" or "unclean," but I know the bias, intended and unintended, of living in almost exclusively white neighborhoods most of my life. The method has been called "close reading" or "engaged reading" as one slows down, attentive to words, movement, and rhetorical artistry—*how* the writer engages us as readers.

The list can go on . . . and the lessons are many. If I superimpose my culturally middle-class American thinking on Scripture as lived out in first-century Palestine in a Jewish and Roman context, I will surely miss something. For example, when Jesus says we are to hate father and mother, I will not understand the Middle Eastern sense of exaggeration and use of hyperbole to say to Jesus' followers: you must be committed to Jesus first and foremost. I will hear teachings about slavery filtered through the American experience of slavery just as I will listen to rhetoric about sexuality through my own lived experience, without wondering how it might have been different in the first century or for centuries before. Truth may be objective but our reading and interpretation is subjective, which requires two practices: humility and reading with others, listening together and allowing others' thoughts to sit at table with ours.

ANOTHER WAY OF LISTENING: PRACTICING HISTORICAL IMAGINATION

Creating or practicing historical imagination is something to be undertaken with humility and always sparking a sense of curiosity to ask, "I wonder how that story is different from mine?" Nigerian Chimamanda Ngozi Adichie had an insightful TED Talk on "The Danger of a Single Story." In it she cautioned us to find the story of others as a way to enable us to celebrate the rich tapestry of our humanity in its uniqueness and healing glory.[8] When we believe truth is contained in a single interpretation of a single story we are in danger of normalizing our own reading in ways that flatten our experience. A single story creates stereotypes that are not necessarily not true, but are incomplete. "They make one story become the only story." Perhaps that's another reason the gospel is given to us in four Gospels, not all of which align perfectly in chronology or text. And yet . . . we can practice historical and cultural imagination with curiosity and the tools of listening for what we don't already understand.

I taught community courses on the parables and said to each class, "If you think you understand the parable completely or identity with the 'hero' in Jesus' story, then you need to go back and listen again—you have probably missed the point." Along with studying grammar, vocabulary, and history, we will learn to be curious about culture, family, mores, and context. Kenneth Bailey is one writer to whom you can listen. *Jesus Through Middle Eastern Eyes* is an excellent resource.

Woman in Gold is the story of a Jewish woman, Maria Altman, played by Helen Mirren, forced to leave Austria because of Nazi threats to her people. Years later, her mission was to reclaim a painting of her Aunt Adele, stripped directly off the walls of her family home by Nazis. Frequently throughout the story the filmmakers moved Maria, from her life in the late 1990s back in her memory to the 1940s. At the conclusion of the film the cinematic timing is perfect. She walks from a room in present day through an entryway into what was once her family home and into the past. It is seamless. At one moment she is on the street in present time and moments

---

8. Adichie, "Danger of a Single Story."

later she walks into the room as it was in her young age. She sees her wedding dance, her parents, her father at his cello, her new husband dancing with family and friends in a Jewish wedding celebration. In her memory the past that was and the present that is become one and the same. When we read with historical imagination we too enter the rooms of the past, seeing them as stories that have become ours. It's easier to do when the story is one of triumph, harder when the story is one of betrayal. We have become familiar with movies as they engage us as viewers in ways that draw us into emotions not ours, emotional memories lived in the cast of characters, tears, joy, grief, sorrow, suffering, and pain, which we experience vicariously on the screen. I feel pain not my own but made mine as I experience the story of biblical people by reading in this way. It can be learned.

I continue to point us to return to a biblical view of sacred purpose. You can hear the assumption in that presupposition: We have wandered away from Scripture, traded it in for North American individualism and thus muted a rich heritage of wisdom on identity and purpose. Returning to a biblical view realigns some of life's most repeated and important questions: "Who am I?" "What am I intended to do with my life?"

As biblical illiteracy becomes the norm, even in churches, the alternative biblical narratives that shaped and reshaped people in the past have become increasingly muted and lost. Jesus at the Jordan River is not only an event of vast shaping importance for how he would proceed in his life. It is a narrative of universal human identity—"you are my beloved son, you are my beloved daughter." The narrative of Yahweh providing skins as clothing to cover the nakedness and shame of Adam and Eve is a narrative of the redemptive movement of God toward all creatures. The narrative of three crosses on a Roman hillside is not only a theological statement of atonement but a declaration of the existence of redemptive love as a foundation to the universe. The technical term for this is the principle of dynamic analogy, which allows today's reader of Scripture to see our own story in the story of our spiritual elders. It is the living word of God given not only to the ancients but through their stories for each of us as we practice the daily art of reading well.

And there's the rub, isn't it? I want to live that way—to the glory of God, at my altar in the world, listening to the mind and heart of God with historical imagination, but how can I be sure? What if I get it wrong? What if I listen and end up with only my own words instead of a divine summons? What then? I entered seminary when I thought I should be enrolling in graduate school in history. I didn't know why I was there except I knew I had no inclination to become a preacher. Two years later, I majored in homiletics. "The effort to untangle the human words from the divine seems not only futile to me but also unnecessary since God works with what is. God uses whatever is usable in a life . . . and those who insist on fireworks in the sky may miss the electricity that sparks the human heart. Discernment doesn't require fireworks, but a willingness to listen to whatever voice will speak . . ."[9]

Researchers in adult learning theory confirm the effectiveness of ruminating on one's life story as transformative. Story is a frame that holds life circumstances together. It is a means of understanding what seems to be random at times in either positive or painful events. And yet reading your story is a lot like reading a novel. You look for plot and themes that might seem random but will lead to deep meaning. This kind of reading (listening) is not a religious practice per se, it is a normal human practice in the "thickness of life." There is no formula for this: we listen to our lives in moments of great drama and weight but also in moments as routine and mundane as my Cheerios at breakfast. *One's calling is richly varied and interesting because each calling is itself a story.* Read your story as God is writing it. This is a skill you can practice, a craft you can hone. Now, where do we begin?

This question becomes foundational to finding sacred purpose. Identity is complex and multifaceted. Parker Palmer defines it for us:

> By *identity* I mean an evolving nexus where all the forces that constitute my life converge in the mystery of self: my genetic makeup, the nature of the man and woman who gave me life, the culture in which I was raised, people who have sustained me and people who have done me harm, the good and ill I have done to others and to myself, the experience of love and suffering—and much, much more. In the midst of that complex field, identity is a moving intersection of the inner and outer forces that make me who I am, converging in the irreducible mystery of being human.[10]

---

9. Taylor, *Gospel Medicine*, 118, 120.
10. Palmer, *Courage to Teach*, 13.

On Holy Ground

FACE, PLACE, RACE, GRACE

There are four very important things you have been given that you had nothing to do with—nothing at all. This list came from a sermon by Charles Spurgeon in the 1800s but I first heard it from Pastor James Ford, on the South Side of Chicago—near where I spent the first years of my life. Pastor Ford is an African American pastor who can preach with a passion I have seldom experienced. In his sermon, he asked this penetrating question: "What do you have that matters, that was *not* given to you? That you had absolutely nothing to do with?"

Face refers to your physical being. I did not choose to be three inches shorter than six feet or to have a declining count of hair follicles or to ultimately need four shoulder surgeries, four knee surgeries, and wear glasses. I had absolutely nothing to do with the face I was given or any of the elements of my physical being, whether it was gender, body shape, or healthiness. Born to C. Arthur and Bertha Anderson, I was shaped by DNA that I was given. I have a rare blood type, A, which approximately only 6.3 percent of Americans have. It too is part of my given identity. Most who read these words will not share that with me. I was a faithful blood donor until a medication caused them to deny my donation. I don't know who received my donations of blood—what their politics were or their religion or gender or race. I didn't ask; I gave it because I knew the day might come when I would need it from another too—whether they agreed with my views or not and whether we voted, worshipped or saw the world in the same way. There are things we are given—all of us—important things we share no matter what we believe. But we don't find many who will screen blood donors on the basis of these things. In our moment of greatest need, we find common ground even in our many differences.

Place refers to the location of your childhood story. The neighborhood that was yours, the kind of house, apartment, or housing project you might have lived in, the demographics of your neighborhood. I was born on the South Side of Chicago and grew up in a bungalow of about a thousand square feet for our family of seven. It was a European melting pot neighborhood of Swedish, Irish, Scottish, Italians, Polish, and Dutch. As a child, did I have a say in where we lived then or about the move thirty miles west to an all-white middle/upper-middle class suburb? No, it was given. I did not choose the place my story was engaged, it was given.

Race: I was not given an opportunity to check a box that asked my preference for race, ethnicity, or family. The great sin in racism is the sheer and inexplicable arrogance about one more thing you had nothing to do with acquiring: your race and ethnicity. My ethnicity is Swedish—100 percent. My grandparents came from "the old country" to Chicago, where we first attended a church of bilingual immigrants and first-generation American-born citizens. I now check the box Caucasian, but who I am in racial identity was given. So, how does anyone among us have the audacity to despise people of a different race, ethnicity, or family? Not one of us chose our race at birth: it was given.

And grace: what did I do to make God love me? Nothing. What did I do that sent Jesus to the cross for the redemption of humankind? Again, nothing. By its very definition, grace is gift, just as are face, place, and race. All are given. I had nothing to do with any of them. Neither did you or anyone else. I did nothing to earn the love and grace of Abba, it was freely given to me by God.

So, read your life as story with attention given to each of these: face, place, race, and grace. Your story is a vibrantly living narrative filled with plot, meaning, nuanced details, and the development of characters—most specifically, you. Finding your identity isn't a simple self-discovery process. There is something *previous* to what I think about myself and it is what God thinks of me. That means that everything I think and feel is by nature a response and the one to whom I respond is God.

> Pause for reflection: Write a two-page story of "where I'm from" using face, place, race, and grace to tell the story. Read your story to someone you trust.

7

Who Holds the Pen That Writes Your Story?

You may have heard it said that your task is to define your future, activate your dreams, and "find your bliss." I'd like to change that and say that your life is being co-written with the Holy Spirit in the everyday story in which you live as one chosen by Abba.

WRITTEN BY THE HOLY SPIRIT

JEAN-PIERRE DE CAUSSADE SAID, "The books the Holy Spirit is writing are living and every soul a volume in which the divine author makes a true revelation of his word, explaining it to every heart, unfolding in every moment."[1] Don't rush past what the man says. In your story, God reveals his Word and words to you. In your story, through your story, God's presence comes near even in moments when you don't necessarily "sense" that presence. I don't suggest to anyone that we will sense presence every day, but we can hear Jesus says every day: "Your faith has made you whole." In your story, you listen, alone or with companions, to the living voice of the Holy Spirit in the text of your own life. It's more than poetic metaphor: if

---

1. De Caussade, *Sacrament of the Present Moment*, 7.

Who Holds the Pen That Writes Your Story?

I see my life as story, I am moved to read my life as precious and sacred. I look for signs of the author's pen in events and moments. When I see my life as story, I know it to be an invitation to enter the great adventure, battle, and drama of the unfolding narrative of my life in a world that is inhabited with presence, the voice of God, the ink of God's pen writing your story as you listen and see. And, be clear about this: It is all of those—adventure, battle, and drama. Nobody ever said following Jesus is easy or without cost, only that we will not journey alone.

Perhaps no one has said it better than the Quaker teacher, writer, and philosopher Thomas R. Kelley. See if his words and images resonate within.

> Deep within us all there is an amazing inner sanctuary of the soul, a holy place, a Divine Center, a speaking Voice to which we may continuously return. Eternity is at our hearts, pressing upon our time-worn lives, warming us with intimations of an astounding destiny, calling us home unto itself. It is a dynamic center, a creative Life that presses to birth within us. It is a Light Within which illuminates the face of God and casts new shadows and new glories upon the face of men (and women). It is a seed stirring to life if we do not choke it. It is the Shekinah of the soul, the Presence in the midst.[2]

What captivates my attention from Kelley's words? It is his notion that spirituality is "coming home" to a place where God's presence has life within me and around me. On holy ground. In my early years, I thought spirituality meant prayer, and evangelism and was distinct from school, work, or daily life. Spirituality meant something ethereal rather than ordinary, eternal, apart from time; it meant *somewhere else*, not here in my body, geography, time, and place. I had it turned around. *Spirituality engages time, space, place, body, and yes, our working life, family life, all of life.*

It turns out Jesus invites us to live attentively for what draws us to live into what we are given. A spirituality of vocation is taking a lifelong walk with Abba Father for the sake of others. In fact, it is actively looking to what we might otherwise walk right past in our busyness. It is learning how to live into what is present on the holy ground of our ordinary lives. There's no formula for this, perhaps, except one: an open heart and mind. What do I mean? You stop looking for the story you expect to be yours and open both mind (attentiveness) and heart (willingness to see) to what may be an entirely new and even richer story into which you can live.

2. Kelley, *Testament of Devotion*, 1.

As I wrote those words, I received an email that moved me as I read in his words the essence of this chapter. After the suicide of his very close friend, my friend returned from Europe to the Pacific Northwest to take over the job left vacant by his friend's death. Dawson wrote, "It's not the story I had written out for myself. I'm still learning to let God take the pen out of my hand and pay attention to the story He's writing. I'm still asking him to help me make sense of it and accept it. But I am coming to love His story far more than the one I thought I should have." His email didn't come out a textbook on spirituality, it came out of gritty, painful, and courageous obedience to his God. For some, the words in a book like this may begin to sound aspirational when, in truth, they are confessional, an honest report from someone who has learned to read their life as God is writing, even in the devastation of losing a close friend to suicide.

PARTICULARITY

Eugene Peterson said, "The Bible makes it clear that every time there is a story of faith, it is completely original. God's creative genius is endless. He, never fatigued and unable to maintain the rigors of creativity, does not resort to mass-producing copies. Each life is a fresh canvas on which he uses lines and colors, shades and lights, textures, and proportions that he has never used before."[3] This is the principle of particularity: God has a particular awareness of you, a particular design, purpose, and love for you. *Your sacred design* is given to you through the power of the Holy Spirit—particular forms of calling for you that are not universal: you will be particularized. This must not be discounted: Read your story to find your sacred design.

Take the example of Bono from U2. His words are riveting when you remember the global influence he has in the particularity of his calling. "I'm a musician. I write songs. I just hope when the day is done, I've been able to tear a little corner off of the darkness."[4] What a loss for the world if Bono never recognized that his music can teach us how "to tear a little corner off the darkness." And he says more: "Wherever you see darkness, there is extraordinary opportunity for the light to burn brighter."[5] Is that the best we get? A little corner? A world in which darkness still exists? It turns out, we serve Jesus with our faithfulness; the outcome is not up to us.

3. Peterson, *Run with the Horses*, 13.
4. Nigro, ed., *Spirituality of Bono*, vii.
5. Thrasher, *Bono*.

Who Holds the Pen That Writes Your Story?

What was *set into motion* in creation *continues* in motion. God is creator and sustainer and the remarkable thing is that we're in on it too. Look at the adoration given God in Psalm 65; "You visit the earth and water it, you greatly enrich it; the river of God is full of water; you provide the people with grain, for you have prepared it . . ." Martin Luther then asked how God does the work of providing grain for food for people and for animals. His answer is that God does the work through human hands, farmers who study agronomy, practice agricultural competence, studying the weather, understanding seasons, soil, and seeds.[6]

WHO AM I?

How then do we discern the particular call God has for our lives? Tim Keller sees three factors to consider:[7]

- *Affinity*. What "people-needs" do I resonate with? Start with your own inner affinity for what will bring well-being to people. Are you motivated as a healer, an inventor, artist, or teacher?
- *Ability*: you ask, "What are my abilities and definite skills? What am I good at?" In my father's family there were three brothers. Grandpa was a builder with great natural skill for making the houses he constructed on the South Side of Chicago. Two of his sons were graced with those same skills in carpentry, design, and construction. None of those skills found their way to me. I jokingly say my primary skill in the building trades is demolition.
- *Opportunity*: "Where does the community tell me I am needed?" Their recognition of my gifts may well be the voices God uses to summons us to worthy dreams.

I had the rare privilege of getting to know the spiritual teacher Henri Nouwen when I was a young pastor in Tacoma, Washington. I heard him speak once for two hours without any notes. We were mesmerized because he spoke to us from his brilliant mind, yes, but thoroughly from his heart. "Our life is trying to answer our most basic question, 'who am I?'"[8] Consider these answers.

---

6. Luther, *Kritische Gesamtausgabe*, 495–96.
7. Keller, *Redefining Work*.
8. Nouwen, "You Belong to God."

I am what I do is one response. What gives me value? Success, productivity, doing big things, my trophies, what Bruce Springsteen called "Glory days"? As long as I have success, all is well. Can you produce and achieve? That must be who you are. The question many fear to ask, however, is, "What happens when I'm no longer Coach, Doc, a teacher, mechanic, you fill in the blank: *Who am I when I am no longer able to do what I do?*"

I am what I possess. What defines me? My possessions, what I own. It may be financial success, a robust IRA account, or the best house, car, or education. But it may be threatened by the passing of time. My itemized spreadsheet of possessions may include something I no longer possess—time. What then? Who am I when I am no longer as capable as I once was or what I possess is compromised by the quick passage of time?

I am what other people tell me I am or what they say about me.[9] I am what other people value, honor, or recognize. And, what if that doesn't happen? If what other people tell me is "You'll never reach your potential." Or, "You'll always be destructive." Or—fill in the blanks from the critical voices who shame you, discount, demean and crush your self-esteem or maybe worse, when they no longer "see" you or value you as they once did. Who am when I feel marginalized, shamed, and disregarded?

For Nouwen, these are all false narratives and incomplete answers. Without success, wealth, or reputation, who am I? Perhaps because he spent years of ministry working in a center for disabled adults, Nouwen himself faced the questions. The friends he made with disabled people transformed him. For Henri one other option is offered. It isn't something you can achieve, produce, or create because you have already received it. Your identity is already given in a most remarkable, unexpected, and unearned way. You have already been given your true identity as the beloved child of God.

Scripture doesn't use the language that Nouwen, Thomas Merton, or Brennan Manning used about the false or the imposter self. The Bible talks more about "missing the mark," which is another way to say "sin." To live in sin is to give credence to what some now call "the false self" or "your imposter self." The false self lives out of fear and shame, preoccupied with acceptance and a need for approval. The false self is often compulsively busy, seeking meaning and belonging through status, money, power, and self-importance; it craves attention and often continues to live out of past trauma and childhood hurt. "While the imposter draws his (her)

---

9. Nouwen, *In the Name of Jesus*, 58.

identity from past achievements and the adulation of others, the true self claims identity in its belovedness . . . God created us for union with Himself . . . Living in awareness of our belovedness is the axis around which the Christian life revolves."[10]

How do we define the self? It's one of the intriguing questions studied for decades. The self is an interaction of at least six things.

1. *Gifts or strengths*: what you have that is natural.
2. *Temperament*: emotional intelligence and competence.
3. *Abilities*: creative, artistic, emotional, logical/rational, mechanical, relational, visual, kinesthetic, or musical.
4. *Experiences*: what has shaped, misshaped, and formed you.
5. *Capacities*: abilities for problem-solving, rational thought, logical competence, generosity, working with numbers, equipment or machinery, an unending list of human capacities. Capacity means the ability to use or process information to make a decision and communicate it accurately to others, and the power to learn and retain knowledge.
6. *Aspirations*: what do you hope for, long for, aspire to, desire?

With such a formidable list, it is evident that one's story can take limitless possible directions. But discerning one's identity is more than an exercise in self-awareness. It is the lifelong practice of paying attention, another way to describe prayer, something many of us struggle to practice. "Prayer . . . is waking up to the presence of God no matter where I am or what I am doing. When I am fully alert to whatever or whoever is right in front of me; when I am electrically aware of the tremendous gift of being alive; when I am able to give myself wholly to the moment I am in, then I am in prayer. Prayer is happening, and it is not necessarily something that I am doing. God is happening, and I am lucky enough to know that I am in The Midst."[11]

Gail Godwin wrote in *Evensong*, "Something's your vocation if it keeps making more of you."[12] We aim for commitments in life that generate and discipline our passion and make more of us than if we simply sit on the sidelines, detached from the fray. The other side of Godwin's understanding

---

10. Manning, *Abba's Child*, 50.
11. Taylor, *Altar in the World*, 178.
12. Godwin, *Evensong*, 12.

is that something is your vocation if it does not lead to the diminishment of you, your values, gifts, or core human identity. It makes sense, as well, that we avoid those vocations that are likely to "make less of us."

> In what ways do your life choices make more of you? In what ways have your choices led to the diminishment of who you are? Have you ever written a statement of life purpose? It's a good exercise if you can be honest with yourself and accountable to others who know you well. What would you include in a purpose statement you could declare freely to others? Take time to write a one-page statement of life purpose.

WORKING THE GEOGRAPHY OF YOUR SOUL

I take you back to *Jayber Crow*. In the middle of the book, Berry contrasts two men, both farmers, one young, one old, one traditional and the other modern. Athey Keith is the old farmer. He is also the father-in-law of the young farmer, Troy Chatham. Read carefully and you discover two differing ways of understanding a spirituality of vocation by contrasting two very different approaches to how we work.

> In coming to the Keith place, he had come into an order that perhaps he did not even recognize. Over a long time, the coming and passing of several generations, the old farm had settled into its patterns and cycles of work—its annual plowing moving from field to field; its animals arriving by birth or purchase, feeding, and growing, thriving, and departing. Its patterns and cycles were virtually the farm's own understanding of what it was doing, of what it could do without diminishments. The farm, so to speak, desired all of its lives to flourish. Athey was not exactly, or not only, what is called a "landowner." He was the farm's farmer, but also its creature and belonging. He lived its life, and it lived his; he knew that, of the two lives, his was meant to be the smaller and the shorter. Of all this, Troy had no idea, not a suspicion. He thought the farm existed to serve and enlarge him . . . Troy went into debt and bought his new equipment because he didn't want to be held

back by demanding circumstances. He was young and strong and ambitious. He wanted to be a star.[13]

What Athey understood from a lifetime of working the land is that his work was not a right so much as privilege. It was not only about himself but about the land itself for him and for those who would follow. It was not something he owned but lived in even as it lived its own life in and around him. Speed, efficiency, haste, and mechanization would not ultimately speed up the growth of seeds into corn or colts into horses or eggs into chickens. Athey seemed to know there is something of the mystery of *Kairos* time—the right moment, the moment of completion, of waiting for the growth to be birthed. By contrast, young Troy Chatham saw the land as merely a commodity, a tool, or an asset to be used purely for his own benefit. For Athey, the land had spiritual meaning, but for Troy the land was nothing more than a means to an end. Athey understood the meaning of membership in a community—with other farmers, with the land, and with the future. Troy saw himself as an individual, a competitor, an independent operator.

Many people I know look at their life with a vision for "changing the world." A great purpose: but where do we begin? I say start in your own corner of the kingdom at your own altar in the world. Get up every morning and consider what waits ahead on the holy ground of your sacred journey in the "small moments of today." I know people like that. For eighteen years I helped teach a class on vocation, ministry, and neighborhoods in the inner city of Chicago. We were mostly bus drivers, it seems, who transported hundreds of students to sit in the presence of people who knew themselves to be called to their jobs, their neighborhood, and their place in God's world. We met lawyers, city council members, teachers, bookkeepers, health care clerks, as well as doctors and nurses, coaches, cooks, artists, and more. Our students were frequently surprised by what they heard because they didn't hear it primarily from clergy but from everyone else. We heard repeatedly that God was already there ahead of us in this neighborhood and ready to call people to work in a challenging part of the city for the sake of others.

I know students who saw a burning bush that burned brightly enough until they heard the voice of God calling them to unexpected holy ground. Dave and Joscey raised their kids in a neighborhood known for gang violence and drugs. Chad went to work teaching immigrants to drive cars in

---

13. Berry, *Jayber Crow*, 182.

a local cemetery! Scott went to Denver to work in an urban center. Chad and Sheila went to work in rural Mississippi. Others set up organizations to create medical clinics, offer affordable loans, research clean water, become therapists or coaches to inspire and train. Most went home with eyes opened to their own sacred purpose. On the way to their ordinary tasks, they discovered a vocation they had unknowingly anticipated all their lives. It is not unexpected then that we are sometimes surprised by where our story takes us.

Pause for reflection: God's voice is revealed in your story . . .

- In our circumstances: what do you hear when you listen to the details of your busy life?

- In the testimony of your heart: What do you hear when you listen to what is deep within?

- In the testimony of your community: what do you hear when you pay attention to voices of wisdom, from your community, church, elders, mentors, and friends?

- In those who have given witness through their life: who has had a significant influence on your own view and relationship with God?

- In holy Scripture: what do you hear when you listen to the foundational guidance of biblical teachings?

8

If You Knew All of My Story . . .

You may have heard it said that your vocation is fostered by success, victories, your "glory days." I'd like to change that to say sacred purpose is fostered by the whole of your story, including shadows, failures, contradictions, wrong steps, and shipwrecks.

Ring the bells that still can ring. Forget your perfect offering.
There is a crack, a crack in everything. That's how the light gets in.
—Leonard Cohen

What if Cohen is right? What if our brokenness, our cracks, let "the light get in"? He may be talking about your story. N. T. Wright translates a verse in 2 Corinthians with unforgettable imagery: "You are a letter of Christ, prepared by us, written not with ink but the Spirit of the living God, not on tablets of stone but on tablets of human hearts. The personal presence and activity of Jesus Christ comes to live within them. They become a letter of Christ to the world. They begin to embody Christ to the world"[1] (2 Corinthians 3:3).

---

1. Wright, *Reflecting the Glory*, 16.

On Holy Ground

Her name was Kathy. Her tired eyes spoke of a life filled with more than her twenty-two years should have known. She came to worship one Sunday with her four children. She sat in the back of the sanctuary and it was evident to me she was not used to sitting in church on a Sunday morning. It was a Communion Sunday and I noticed she did not accept the bread and the cup when they were offered. Later I visited her in a rundown apartment that hadn't known upkeep for some time. The living room was cluttered with children's things and I was invited to sit in the only chair. She used a child's stool as we talked.

Eventually, I asked her about Communion and she said, "Oh, no, I could never be worthy enough. If you knew all of my story, you would understand." I asked, "Can you tell me your story?" I asked as gently as I could. Slowly she began to talk about her addiction to cocaine and her life of moving from place to place. She told me each of her children had a different father and about her recent arrest. The father of her youngest child forced her at gunpoint to sell drugs to pay for his habit. The arrest, she said, helped her find the courage to walk through the doors of the church. She knew she was facing the devil and couldn't do it alone. Did you hear her words? It took trauma in her life to find the courage to walk through the doors of the church.

I told her what I knew of Jesus and grace, forgiveness, and redemption. I came back with furniture, clothes, and a bit of money to help. A few months later I sat in the courtroom for her trial. The judge noticed me talking to her and invited me to identify myself and then to sit at the defense table with her. When it was time for him to make his judgment, he looked and me and said, "Pastor, if you sat on my side of the bench, what would you decide?" I rose to my feet, heart pounding, my brain scrambling for words until they flowed without hesitation. In that moment, I was given words not my own: "Your honor, this woman's name is Kathy. You could call her what she is—a user of drugs, a felon, a criminal. I would ask you instead to use her other names: daughter, mother, a determined, courageous young woman committed to her children, ready to finish rehab and battle all of this with the help of a church beside her. I would ask you to call her by name, give her probation, and send her home today to her children." That afternoon, Kathy heard her name called by the name God would use— my child, my beloved, my daughter. Finally the judge raised his gavel and said, "It is so ordered as the pastor has said. Probation, drug rehabilitation, and she is released to return home to her children." The next Sunday was Communion Sunday. Seated in the front row of the sanctuary was a young woman with her four children. When she was offered the bread and the cup, she cradled them in her hands and received the body and blood of Christ. She understood: God believes in her.

"The glory of Christ is not revealed in a spectacular show of success, in people who get everything right all the time...The church reveals the glory of Christ through suffering and shame as much as through what the world counts as success... The church is called to be where the world is in pain, at the place where the world is suffering and in a state of shame and sorrow. The church is there as the presence of the suffering Christ in the world..."[2]

"We have this treasure in clay jars—the treasure of this gospel, the light shining out of darkness to give knowledge of the glory of God. We are battered old flowerpots filled with the glory of God, so that it is quite clear that the power and the glory belong to God, not to us... We can be people who embody the gospel of Jesus Christ only if we are people who go through suffering, danger, difficulty, and failure."[3] I can't know what your story of hurt and brokenness is, but I can join both Paul and N. T. Wright to welcome you to a community of imperfection. Are you surprised to read Wright's words above? We don't merely rub shoulders with people hiding their pain. We are those treasures in fragile earthen clay jars too. Made from the earth, as was Adam, the "creature of the earth," we are made a treasure through our identity as the beloved. Many of us put our best energy into avoiding the truth that we are not only sent to bring healing to the broken but to receive it for ourselves. We cannot give to others what we have not received for ourselves.

> Pause for reflection: "If you knew my whole story, you'd understand." Have you ever said those words to anyone? Do you know someone who has? Can you identify why people might feel that way? What has happened in your life to cause you to feel that way?

Dan Allender is one of our best teachers about story, trauma, and recovery. He offers a snapshot of how to get started on the process for yourself:

> Hang out with people who are confident of the wild goodness of Jesus and who aren't apt to offer quick or silly and superficial

---

2. Wright, *Reflecting the Glory*, 19.
3. Wright, *Reflecting the Glory*, 32.

solutions to life's struggles. These people are more often than not curious to the bone about the human heart, voracious readers of fiction, lovers of theatre, and absolutely intrigued by the heart of Jesus. If you can find this pearl of a person—a counselor, a sage, or just a compassionate friend—then tell him (her) a single story of some event that deeply shaped who you are. Choose a story that bears heartache in a highly formative period of life. Let your friend listen and feel your story and then let him (her) pursue understanding through conversation. Take it in. Give all the new thoughts to Jesus. Invite him into the heartache with you.[4]

SACRED HISTORY

Dallas Willard speaks directly to an irrefutable spiritual context: "Transformation is actually carried out in our real life, where we dwell with God and our neighbors . . . God has yet to bless anyone except where they actually are."[5] In many biblical stories, our ancestors were surprised by the twists and turns of "real" life. My favorite is Jacob. He was a serial deceiver who stole the birthright from his brother and found himself on the run from Esau's rage and threats. He came to a place of darkness and slept that night on the cold, hard ground, using, of all things, a stone as his pillow. Hardly a night for comfortable REM sleep, but he dreamed deeply and what he heard astonished him as the voice of God. "Know that I am with you and will keep you wherever you go and will bring you back to this land; for I will not leave you until I have done what I have promised you" (Genesis 28:15). Instead of judgment, he was given a future; instead of condemnation, hope. He awoke and declared words spoken in surprise. "Surely the Lord was in this place—and I did not know it . . . This is none other than the house of God, and this is the gate of heaven" (Genesis 28:16–17). Did I mention that he slept on the ground? Remarkable! He called the place Beth-El, the "house of God."

You know the song "We are climbing Jacob's Ladder." But can you hear it, truly? This is not a song about Jacob and his magnificent faith. He didn't even see or know God's presence until after the fact. But he eventually did get it. He understood, *eventually*, that God came into the place and time in his life even when he didn't catch on at first. God "was in this place." And in

4. Allender, "Understanding Your Story."
5. Willard, *Divine Conspiracy*, 347–48.

yours and mine. Does that mean it will always happen that way? Of course not. But it does mean that we can find transformation when we discern the already active presence of God even in a desert of despair, fear, and desperation, "on the run."

Jacob's story was transformed by a dream of God's presence. When he awoke, nothing in the world would ever look the same to him. In time, God changed Jacob's name to Israel. His children became the twelve tribes of Israel, and Jacob bowed in worship of Yahweh. Gracious to Jacob, God's love transformed him from deceiver to a leader of people. Knowing himself beloved by God through such acts of grace, Jacob became a participant in restorative justice with Esau. He said, "Truly to see your face is like seeing the face of God since I have received such favor" (Genesis 33:10). Can it be true? To see the face of God in the face of an enemy, an estranged brother, is a pathway to reconciliation? Jacob would say, "Yes!" Jesus challenges our disengaged discipleship. He confronts our tendency to love only those within our tribe and ideological identity. Jesus transforms our self-defined spirituality because he preached something robust, inclusive, generous, redemptive, compassionate, and nuanced.

ROOTS, BRANCHES, FRUIT

Are you aware how often Jesus spoke about spirituality in such terms? He knew our stories are truly rooted within all that we have lived: joy, sorrow, delight, despair, success, failure, pleasure, and pain. We are rooted as well in our families of origin, with all the beauty and pain families bring. But we, as North Americans, don't like to spend time looking at roots—we only want to see the fruit, the flowers, and the beauty, but none of that can be known without the roots planted in soil. We are wrong to call it *dirt* because *soil* is a living organism and the source of our growth. So, we tend to see only what is above ground and visible, and not what is below the surface. I returned to campus one fall and saw a tree that I loved lying on its side, the root ball still below ground but the tree had been cut down. In that moment I understood: the tree was already dead but didn't yet know it. Without the roots, how long until the leaves would die? In that moment it still looked vigorous, healthy, and green, but, in reality, it was already dying. That's a word of caution for us in the Western culture where we seem to be increasingly severed from our roots. What is below ground that we cannot see is sometimes as big as what is above ground that we can see. God doesn't just work at the surface level but deep below in our roots, the stories of our past, the pain and often the damage that has been done *to* us and, truthfully, done *by* us. Those roots carry our stories, our treasure, and our trauma. Below the surface are the stories that we must courageously read. As you read your story, you encounter your own emerging identity not only in your gifts, strengths, and aptitudes, but in all the ways your humanity has been formed, tested, failed, and betrayed. It's all there. You do not get to maturity without shadows, darkness, suffering, and pain. You come against walls and limitations, you find holes in your soul that have come from trauma and failure imposed by others and self-imposed.

At a family reunion in Minnesota my granddaughter, Laine, was frustrated. When we arrived at our fishing spot, Sloane, our oldest granddaughter, cast her line and immediately hauled in a walleye pike. She threw out her line a second time with the same result. And then a third time. By then, we were all feeling a bit jealous. Sloane was the only one in the boat catching fish, while the rest of us caught nothing. Laine made her feelings known, loudly enough for all to hear. "Nothing is happening," she lamented with some frustration. Truthfully, we all felt it. But Bruce, my friend and our wise guide, said, "You know, Laine, it may seem that nothing is happening, but down below, deeper, a great deal is happening." Soon after she caught her first fish.

Dawson and Laurel Jones wrote with insight in their blog: "He (Abba) is the great cartographer . . . He knows the way home. In a crazy twist, he moved into our neighborhood to dwell in us, to make us his home. It is good then to let him lead us home. There is no home apart from him. And though he leads us, it is also our good Father who will be there when we arrive. If you ask them and anyone who has stepped into the storms of tragedy, intense sorrow, physical or emotional catastrophe you will hear them say: 'we had no road map, we had no tools, we had no step one.'"[6] But, Dawson and Laurel would tell you, they had what could give them hope enough to find a way through the darkest of times: they lived in relationship with Abba, the map-maker, who knows the way home.

And, here's something to understand: we all are on a journey "to be seen." As a five-year-old in a house of five children, I wandered next door to see Bill and Tine. He was my hero, a Chicago motorcycle cop. Pretendingly, he put me in jail, fingerprinted me, and let me climb the bars until more serious criminals arrived to occupy what had become my play space for a short time. He seemed to enjoy this young, talkative little boy and often

---

6. Jones and Jones, *Finding God in the Geography of our Hearts*, 1.

took me up the street to the tavern. My parents were teetotalers so this frequent expedition surprises my memory but I have vivid memories of entering the dark interior of a Chicago tavern with the smell of cigarettes, beer, and whiskey. Bill would prop me up on a barstool, order my 7-Up, light up his unfiltered Camel cigarette and listen... to me. He and Tine had no children so perhaps I was a substitute they could enjoy just long enough to happily return me home. But in any event my childhood story includes that tavern as a kind of sanctuary for my soul—somehow I mattered to Bill, somehow I was cared for in his way. To be seen is an inherent human need. Discerning identity starts with being seen. My story includes the most vivid memories as a child spending time in, of all places, a smoky tavern perched in my habitual seat, next to the Irish cop whom I adored. That is part of my spiritual formation and my story, as much as attending worship services just a few miles from there.

NOTHING'S EVER WASTED: IS THERE A PLAN B?

What if plan A collapses along with your dreams, training, and expectations? Few things are as painful. We ask: Did I get the vision wrong? Did I misread God's intentions for my story? Can I recover from such sharp disappointment? You can. How? Step into the life of ancient Israel with historical imagination.

The people of Israel were in exile in Babylon. Exile is a place of disappointment and failed dreams, a place where you are not "at home" with your present situation, a place where you don't feel you belong. Not only homelessness, but "exile" creates a sense of hopelessness, impotence, and uncertainty... you feel yourself away from having control over your story and your future. Israel knew exile. We too may have our own experience of *exile*, where our emotional and spiritual stories don't leave us feeling "at home." In such times, the temptation is to become self-preoccupied. We are no longer attentive and alert to what might be right before our eyes. The loss of a dream can freeze us into what feels like failure. It looks and feels like nothing good is happening.

And something more: for some, many even, there is a belief there is no longer anything sacred. If I believe God has abandoned me or that God doesn't exist at all, what's left to create sacred purpose? In the return to "the promised land," a first step by Ezra was to build a tower and read Torah to people, to call the people who had lived in exile to remember that God's love is *hesed* or always faithful, always loyal to covenant. Do you see what he did? He called his people to remember Torah (Scripture) in order to return to faithfulness to God. Whatever we thought was plan A may need to transform to something else, but not something less.

Yahweh had a plan for Israel. You might call it plan B. Through young Jeremiah, God told them they would have to wait to return to Jerusalem from their exile in Babylon—seventy years, in fact. But then, plan B: "For surely, I know the plans I have for you, says the Lord, plans for your welfare and not for harm, to give you a future with hope. Then when you call upon me and come and pray to me, I will hear you. When you search for me, you will find me, if you seek me with all your heart, I will let you find me, says the Lord . . ." (Jeremiah 29:11-12). Israel returned home from exile and so will you as you continue to read the story God is writing. God's presence often comes as simple encouragement and sometimes a call to patience.

I was on a Zoom call with a trusted friend, holding the draft of this book in my hands. She looked me in the eye and said words not often heard by any of us: "Keith, this is your most important work." Her words were a true encouragement, giving me confidence to keep going with the task at hand. It felt as though God's voice was speaking through her, echoing with affirmation and strengthening my trust in the process. Brennan Manning was another such voice in my life. I had the great good gift of friendship with him, this former priest, author, speaker and, yes, alcoholic. He was a character who would show up to chapel in tattered jeans with patches, because he saw himself and all of us, frankly, as ragamuffins. He understood that Jesus loves ragamuffins and titled one of his books *The Ragamuffin Gospel*. He didn't like to eat before he preached but he loved two things after: brownies and ice cream. I bought him half a dozen brownies one day after he preached in chapel. He ate them all. By his preaching, books, phone calls, and thoughtful questions, he was a voice from the balcony for me, cheering me to go forward, stay the course, and trust that God has more to say to all of us when we listen with the same careful attention people like Brennan. He as much as anyone in my life has shown me the face of God, spoken the voice of God to me, and healed my soul in its most shaky moments. How did he do this? He saw me, cherished me somehow, listened to me as I spoke in my own stuttering way about God to him. There is no nourishment that sustains as does this kind of love in the brightest and darkest of times. Even in the darkness, we are sustained to know that God has not and never will abandon us. "I am with you always," said Jesus (Matthew 28:20).

9

Heartbreak and Shipwrecks

You may have heard it said that failure, heartbreak, and shipwrecks lead to despair. I want to change that and say failure and tragedy may also navigate us to new shores of hope and purpose.

LISTENING DEEPLY REQUIRES THAT we listen even in times of heartbreak and pain. My own narrative of pain began before I was born, when the life-shaping heartbreak of my life occurred. My older brother—firstborn—preceded me by five years. At the moment of his birth, just days before the actual delivery, my mother went into seizures that cut off the oxygen flow to his prenatal brain, causing brain damage. They wouldn't know until a bit later, but he was what they then sadly called *retarded*. His disability would freeze his mental acuity at about the age of a six-year-old. He grew tall and strong—he could have been a fine athlete, but that was not to be. My experiences with Jerry included sharing a bedroom until I was a senior in college, sharing matching Schwinn bicycles—and we shared a father, whose answer to my requests for time were most often, "Sure, let's get Jerry to come along too."

My heartbreak was the natural consequence of being a middle child—the healthy, loud, active only other son in a family of five children. In the 1950s they mainstreamed Jerry in the so-called "special class" comprised of variously disabled and mentally challenged children. The polite word used was "special." Sadly, because they were "special," they were treated badly by the rest of the school, unfamiliar with children who couldn't speak articulately, or who drooled or were excessively loud and unpredictable, who laughed when it was the wrong moment and who didn't seem to hear the words I heard as we walked through town—"retard" being the most frequent and loudest of the invectives. To the family heartache, I added my own embarrassment at times, that I should be saddled with such a burden. Later, the heartache of my life was the shame that would be added to my young soul knowing that I didn't always stand up for Jerry well. There were noble moments too, I suppose, when I stood tall in the face of the cruel words and actions of kids and adults, including most often, parents, when I told them to back off, shut up (forbidden in my household), and otherwise defended my brother.

Whatever my own heartbreaks, I return again and again to two immigrants' children, my young mother and father. Their firstborn was Jerry. It took just a few short years to realize his birth trauma was permanent; their heartache would be lifelong. Imagine all their dreams wrapped up and dashed in the words of the doctor who had to tell them the news of brain damage. My mother didn't talk easily about her emotions, but twenty years before her death she wrote a poem. She called it a psalm. We published it at her funeral. As I write this, Jerry is still alive. Mom and Dad cared and provided for him all the days of their lives. There are shadows of darkness that come to every life. Some are fleeting like a burst of sunlight that flashes across a room followed by clouds. Some last a lifetime of sadness, disappointment, and heartbreak felt most intensely by those with broken dreams. And yet, even in light of his limited intellect, Jesus has shown Jerry his true identity and Jerry can say it, sing it, and confess it in childlike conviction: "Jesus loves me, this I know."

> I praise you, Lord
> for your loving kindness
> and mercy to me.
> I thank you Lord
> for giving me life
> and then the gift of eternal life.
> I thank you now for these years
> in which you have graciously meted out what was best for me.
> Lord, you know I wouldn't have
> chosen the hard things, but I thank you for being at my side every day.
> Great is my God and worthy to receive praise.
> —Bertha Marion Liljedahl Anderson

DAILY EXAMEN: CONSOLATION AND DESOLATION

I don't know how Mom coped with five children including a special needs oldest son. But I know her faith was witnessed in the psalm she wrote. She lived into the dailiness of her life's challenges and the story that was her life. An ancient spiritual practice is especially useful in learning to read *all* your life as story—it's called an examen, sometimes practiced daily. It is a simple reflection on the day just past. You recall events and feelings, noticing where you experienced God's presence or sensed guidance from the Spirit. It is a practice that has roots in the work of Ignatius of Loyola in the sixteenth century. Ignatius understood that you need margins in your calendar if you want to read God's movement in your story. The daily examen is one way to create space to listen for respite, peace, and comfort.

Traditionally there are five movements in the examen. You typically begin with a brief prayer that acknowledges a desire for God's presence, followed with a word of gratitude that asks, "For what am I grateful this day?" The examen ends with a prayer about tomorrow: what do you hope to see happen then? In between the prayers are steps that include two of the most important concepts in the examen: *consolation* and *desolation*. They alert us to how God might be working in our story in two very different ways:

> *Consolation* is an experience that causes you to feel fully alive, at peace, joyful, happy, comforted, whole, connected, your best self, etc., and could be understood as an experience in which you feel close to God.
>
> *Desolation* is an experience that causes you to feel drained of energy, frustrated, irritated, angry, sad, sorrowful, alone, isolated, unaccepted, fragmented, less than your best self, etc., and could be understood as an experience in which you feel far away from God.[1]

I sat with the director of a local theater in Seattle who spoke at our faculty retreat. One line captured my imagination. "A lighting designer is also a shadow designer." It was a profound thought. We live in both light and shadows. These words are exceptionally important to hear: "Christians seldom sing in the minor key. We fear the somber; we seem to hold sorrow in low-esteem . . . failing to see that doubt and despair are the dark soil that is necessary to grow confidence and joy."[2]

---

1. See Thibodeaux, *Examen*.
2. Allender, *Hidden Hope of Lament*.

On Holy Ground

Does it surprise you to hear that God already knows about tragedy in your life and intends to transform it? Anne Lamott adds, "We learn through pain that some of the things we thought were castles turn out to be prisons and we desperately want out, but even though we built them, we can't find the door. Yet maybe if you ask God for help in knowing which direction to face, you'll have a moment of intuition. Maybe you'll see at least one next right step you can take."[3] Suffering shipwrecks and knowing heartbreak creates one of our most feared emotions: we sense the loss of control and few of us live well feeling out of control. Can it be that is the very purpose of suffering, to teach us how to surrender our spirits to Jesus?

Sharon Daloz Parks writes about the transformative role of shipwrecks.

> If we do survive shipwreck—if we wash up on a new shore, perceiving more adequately how life really is—there is gladness. It is gladness that pervades one's whole being; there is a new sense of vitality, be it quiet or exuberant. Usually, however, there is more than relief in this gladness. There is transformation. We discover a new reality behind the loss . . . As the primal, elemental force of promise stirs again within us, we often experience it as a force acting upon us, beneath us, carrying us, sometimes in spite of our resistance into a new meaning, new consciousness, new faith.[4]

We don't always know it at first, but wounding leads to God. Incredibly, the word "innocence" means "not wounded yet."[5] Anne Lamott struggles with the clichéd answers people give to tragedy. She is wisely human to reject easy answers to overwhelming human disaster. She said, "I asked a wise friend, 'Is there meaning in what happened in the slaughter at the Sandy Hook school in Newtown?' He said, '*not yet.*'"[6] It's a powerful word, is it not? We don't have easy answers for tragedies of unspeakable violence. My family experienced that in the recent death of a beloved niece. The violence was an assault by a former boyfriend on Katie's friend who was with her to protect her. A knife was pulled and Katie's friend was brutally murdered. Katie blamed herself. Her words to her mother were, "It's all my fault." Three days later, Katie's body was found in her apartment, with her dead of an accidental overdose. Our grief was intense: It gutted us. We know too well: A single phone call can be devastating and bring horrifying news

---

3. Lamott, *Stitches*, 14–15.
4. Parks, *Big Questions, Worthy Dreams*, 29.
5. Rohr, *True Self, False Self*.
6. Lamott, *Help, Thanks, Wow*, 37.

of the worst kind. All I know is that we cannot escape the sheer unrelenting pain of suffering that comes from such grief. Is there life after such horror? "Not yet." But my faith says *there is life beyond* . . . I hold on to that belief. I can only sustain that faith because I am a prisoner of hope (Zechariah 9:12, KJV). I can only persist in that belief because I know the biblical story of Jesus' life, suffering, crucifixion, death, and resurrection.

Eugene Peterson said it with spare prose: "We live in the reality of both the shadow and the shepherd."[7] "Yea though I walk through the valley of the shadow of death" (Psalm 23:4 KJV) is not an experience unknown to the human family. If we live long enough, we all walk through the valley of the shadow of death. If we live long enough, we will know suffering for which we never signed up. And we will have a decision to make: Will we let God transform us through our struggles? Remember, "We learn through pain that some of the things we thought were castles turn out to be prisons and we desperately want out, but even though we built them, we can't find the door. Yet maybe if you ask God for help in knowing which direction to face, you'll have a moment of intuition. Maybe you'll see at least one next right step you can take."[8]

Heartaches, shipwrecks, and suffering all create loss. Loss takes many forms—loss of security, loss of relationship, loss of health, loss of innocence, and even loss of our dreams. The natural response to loss is grief. We experience sorrow, suffering that is emotional and deeply spiritual, and we long for wholeness, a return to what was ours before. I understand it was said of Anne Frank at one of the concentration camps, "her tears never ran dry." The question is always what follows grief—resentment or gratitude? In resentment we harden our hearts; in gratitude that can only come from faith we open our hearts. In resentment, we mourn what seems terminal in despair; in gratitude we long for hope as we remember our deepest identity as ones beloved by God. We remember that we are not alone even in the worst life can do to us; there is a companion who walks alongside.

One of my most precious possessions is a personal letter from Brennan Manning. We wrote and spoke often during a time of great stress, failure, and pain. Words like his can only come from a fellow "ragamuffin" as flawed and finite as I.

> It is comforting to remember that the terrors of the unknown future are born and nurtured solely by your mind. They do not

---

7. Peterson, *As Kingfishers Catch Fire*, 101.
8. Lamott, *Stitches*, 14.

exist in the mind of God. They have no ontological reality and God cannot deal with what does not exist. What Merton has taught me is simple: live in now and live in mercy. *Thank God for the fall*, because it provides him with the opportunity to do what he likes to do best—show mercy and extend compassion. The failure of some to respond to your hurt is a wound that probably will never close. When in a similar situation, I asked for the grace to turn my resentment into compassion—for their brokenness. In union with Jesus, the wound will bring healing and wholeness to you and others. Friends who stand with you in the bad weather of life are a rare and precious treasure. For your spiritual health, focus more on them than on the fair weather so-called "friends."

In a later letter he gave me a benediction for life: "I pray that as the summer heat intensifies, you get splashed occasionally with a bucket of loving water. Your brother, Brennan."

> Pause for reflection. "Our gifts and wounds are one." Is there unresolved grief in your story? What heartbreaks or shipwrecks have you experienced? Name them—recent past, distant past. How have they limited you? Have they pointed you toward a vocation? Is there debris in your life that clutters the path and limits your ability to seek God's forgiveness? What keeps you from doing that today, now?

WHERE ARE YOU HIDING THE RAINBOW?

I shall never forget the day I received a call from the University of Puget Sound. "Pastor Anderson, I need you to come to my office. One of *your* parishioners needs you right now. It is a crisis." I was not ready for what awaited me. I entered the professor's office to find one of our students in a fetal position underneath the desk. The professor left me alone with a student, whose body was twitching and who spoke not at all. I didn't know how to react. I truly had no idea what to do. I thought back through everything they taught me in seminary and came up blank. I must have skipped class on the what-to-do-when-someone-is-in-a-fetal-position-in-a-faculty-office day! I did the only thing I could think of: I laid on the floor next to her and began to talk very quietly. I stroked her hair and gently rubbed her shoulder and spent nearly an hour telling her stories about conversations we had shared until slowly, timidly she began to speak. The stress was too much and she had panicked. We got her to the hospital and in the weeks that followed, she faced another crisis: What would she do with this embarrassment, failure, and humiliation? She had two options: to allow this to defeat her and cause her to shut the door and live lifelong in a world of defeat, or to grow in compassion. She chose the latter. Through struggle, counseling, and love from a caring community, she found her way back to health and a ministry that is forever enriched by her pain. Suffering changes our priorities and often refocuses our understanding of our purpose. About a year later she wrote:

> God,
> Where are you hiding the rainbow?
> The rainbow is your promise to me that
> you'll never flood the Earth again
> That when it rains You won't desert mankind.
>
> Lord,
> You've brought rain to my life
> To teach me about myself,
> And my relationships to other people
> And how I can best serve You
> By being the me you intended me to be
> But Lord, you've created a flood
> A flood of emotion, of depression, anger, and despair,
> Of searching and questioning into a void
> Where the answers seem so dim and out of reach,
> Lord God, please show me a rainbow
> That I may know you are with me
> And the flood can once again recede
> And I can experience the joy of pure, refreshing, cleansing rain.

That poem was a key step in her recovery. By writing it, she set it down and let go of her humiliation and heartbreak. And *because* of her pain, she became more human, not less. *Because* of her failure, she became more successful, not less. *Because* of her choices, she opened the doors to more of life. She is now more capable than before of sensitive listening and effective caring. She turned this failure into a great formative time of growth. Amanda Gorman also wrote about pain in words that won't let me go:

> Our wounds, too are our windows. Through them we watch the world.[9]

9. Gorman, *Call Us What We Carry*, 43.

On Holy Ground

Our scars are the brightest parts of us.[10]

I met frequently with a student in her late college years. She had suffered abuse and trauma and lived with guilt over it all. We talked about forgiveness and the grace of a loving God. One day she brought me a small clay pot that was disfigured, not broken, but not whole. The top half had collapsed in the oven but she covered it with a beautiful paint as she would a completed pot. "This is from my 'failure' collection," she said. "It reminds me that I am beloved of God even though my story includes times of failure and pain." It has been a most precious icon of the power of God's redemptive love as we answer the call. Maturity comes through storms, failures, grief, limitations, and even depression. It's remarkable to see that God creates life-giving reality even in the midst of moments of heartache and shipwreck—darkness, doubt, anger, fear, grief, shame, rejection, loneliness, and confusion. "We also boast in our sufferings, knowing that suffering produces endurance, and endurance produces character, and character produces hope, and hope does not disappoint us because God's love has been poured into our hearts through the Holy Spirit that has been given to us" (Romans 5:3–5). It comes back, as always, to our identity as the beloved. You may be asking by now, what has this to do with our calling? Everything. The sacred design that is mine has come *because* of my sin, my suffering, and my wounds.

What if that is true? What if I would not be "me" without limitations that have come from wounds, heartbreak, and failure? I thought I would go to seminary, study theology, be given answers and certitude to make me into a competent pastor. But none of that prepared me for death by accident, suicides, drug overdoses, hit-and-run drivers, DUI drivers, house fires that damaged and marred bodies and killed family members, chronic suffering, betrayal, and being let down by life.

A young pastor in a Wendell Berry short story was familiar with suffering too. "His calling, and the respect it accorded to it, admitted him into the presence of troubles he could not mend."[11] These things shaped me as a pastor as they dramatically changed the lives of each person for whom this was their story. Standing with people in emotional pain is what pastors do. And it tears at our hearts. But why should we be surprised? When Jesus heard the news that his dear friend Lazarus had died, his actions showed us

---

10. Gorman, *Call Us What We Carry*, 60.
11. Berry, *Place in Time*, 52.

the heart of God. "Jesus wept." Tears of loss, suffering, and pain. That's not the only time we see Jesus' tears. "As (Jesus) came near and saw the city, he wept over it . . ." (Luke 19:41). Tears for the salvation and restoration of the people. This is the *pathos* of God. It is not "mere emotions," but something in the divine character that moves God to act.

"Because God is creator, He is moved to redeem and restore when He sees the corrosive and destructive effects of evil on His creation. This *pathos* is contrasted with the *apatheia* of the gods early Christianity encountered in the religions of the ancient world. *Apatheia* was their inability to feel or be influenced."[12] In contrast to an *apathetic* God, the God of passion, tears, and love calls us to be present to suffering, ours and others. But it is not our responsibility to bring change. It is our responsibility to live into the same pathos of God. I listened to Bart Campolo in an old sermon say it this way: "There are some people you cannot fix, there are some people you cannot save, there are some people you cannot help, but there's nobody, nobody you can't love."

---

12. Moltmann, *Crucified God*, 270.

10

Seriously God, the Church?
Is That the Best You Could Do?

You may have heard it said that vocation is an aria, your greatest solo performance. I would change that a bit. Vocation is an orchestra of people committed to fidelity in their craft together.

I've heard Eugene Peterson say more than once, "We've lost the pronouns 'we' and 'us.'" That means, to my ears, that community is a song we no longer sing. It is, however, a refrain we need to reclaim in Western culture and especially in the church. God calls us to listen *with* others as a way of life. In his beautiful *African Prayer Book*, Bishop Desmond Tutu understands this better than most. "We say in our African idiom, 'A person is a person through other persons.' . . . God is smart, making us different so that we will get to know our need of one another. We are meant to complement one another in order to be truly human and realize the fullness of our potential to be human. After all, we are created in the image of a God who is diversity of persons in ineffable unity."[1]

---

1. Tutu, *African Prayer Book*, xiv–xv.

SOUL FRIENDS

In my early years in campus ministry, I was asked to form an intramural volleyball team. I did. I was the captain. It was my team. And, I was undoubtedly the least gifted player on the team. But there we were—one game away from winning the championship. Hardly because of my skills, definitely because we learned to play well together. We won the game. And, we needed a team name to go along with our winning jerseys. I talked to Sid, athletic guru of our intramural league. "Do you have any ideas for a great team name?" He looked at me as if what he was about to say was a revelation direct from God. "Soul Friends. That's your name, Soul Friends."

I later learned it is a translation of an Irish word, *anamchara*. It's a rich and evocative image. One writer describes it in a lovely phrase, "compassionate presence."[2] It possibly originated in Irish monastic life, where it referred to a teacher, companion, or spiritual guide, clerical or lay, male or female. This kind of hospitality is a ministry of friends who open lives, homes, and hearts to others for their refreshment, nurture, growth, and enjoyment.[3] Always, it stirs in me a list of those who have been my soul friends, those without whom my spiritual journey would be lonely and missing the grand gift of hospitality from others. There was no agenda. What guided us was friendship, a relationship of companionship through stories, questions, insights, pain, and joy.

Not every conversation is about reading your calling or discerning your vocation. How then does spiritual friendship make a difference? In community we learn to listen *to* each other and to *the voice of God* speaking to us together. We may not be given an answer, we probably will never be given an itinerary, but we can listen better with companions who help us ask our questions and interpret our dreams. Each of us need someone who cares to listen to our story. Soul friendship is also known as theological hospitality, making respectful and open space for others. In hospitality, we treat others as guests, never as strangers, enemies, or adversaries. We needn't agree with all of each other's viewpoints, values, assumptions, or agendas, but we will have learned to imitate Jesus' hospitality in our forms of theological hospitality: we welcome, accept, and seek to love.

> Above all, maintain constant love for one another, for love covers a multitude of sins. Be hospitable to one another without

---

2. Ryan, *Working from the Heart*, 160.
3. Sellner, "Soul Friendship."

complaining. Like good stewards of the manifold grace of God, serve one another with whatever gift each of you has received. Whoever speaks must do so as one speaking the very words of God; whoever serves must do so with the strength that God supplies, so that God may be glorified in all things through Jesus Christ. To God belong the glory and the power forever and ever. Amen. (1 Peter 4:8–11)

Bob Young was the head football coach of the University of Sioux Falls Cougars, a team that won national and regional championships during his years at the helm. In his retirement, after his wife of sixty-plus years, Diane, died, some of his former players made him an offer. It was more like a summons from the Lord himself. They offered to make contact with every player, coach, or friend of USF football during his tenure as coach. "We're not ready to be done and you're not either. We need more of you." Bob asked me to join a Zoom call some months later. I wasn't prepared for the experience. I watched something remarkable. There were about fifty men on the call. It had been many years since I walked the sidelines with Bob, but slowly I began to recognize some of those once young players, now gray-haired, balding, and "seasoned." Bob opened with prayer and then started with his "gallery view" on Zoom. He took time to greet every man by name, asked a question about their faith, job, health, or family, and then on to the next person. He knew each one intimately enough to give them a word from the Spirit—an encouragement or challenge. He finally came to one to whom he said, "It's time for you to get serious about your faith as a mentor of younger guys. They need to know you and hear all of your very challenged story." I had never seen anything like that before. He was pastoral, I suppose, but he was *anamchara* to each one. His words called each to remember these things

- You are beloved of God as evidenced by the cross of Christ.
- Your discipleship to Jesus is the most important thing in your life.
- Your relationships begin with family and your spouse if you are married.
- You are needed by others—at work, your church and community, so get to it!

This is one way God works with us. The Spirit is given to us all, often together. Each man was touched particularly by the spirit and heart of this gracious and truth-telling coach, but we all knew in our own experience that we were touched as well by being part of a community of soul friends, called together on Zoom by the Holy Spirit.

A few months later, Bob was being taken to the hospital by a friend of many years, someone he had helped find his way back to God. Gasping for oxygen, Bob spent his last minutes on earth on the phone, calling some of those same guys, I am sure, with words of encouragement and challenge. He took a couple of calls from others with the same intention: True to his vocation he was a voice of invitation, encouragement, and redemption right up to the end of his days on earth. How do you imagine your last half-hour of life? For Bob it was more of the same faithfulness to his sacred purpose and to Jesus that he had lived all those years I knew him. It's a profound question, is it not? If you could script your last hour on earth, what would you write?

LEADERSHIP OF COMPANIONSHIP

Moses was called by God but not in the way he expected, not to the place he expected, and not for the reasons he expected. After he murdered an Egyptian overseer who was beating one of Moses' fellow Israelites, he covered up the crime and hid the body. But he could not cover up the guilt within and no longer believed he could be a leader of his people. From the palace of the Pharaoh to a shepherd's field, he distanced himself from the fury of his crime until that day he encountered a bush on fire. It wasn't a completely unexpected sight in the desert. Combustion can occur on its own due to heat, sunshine, and sparks from sand and branches flying around—except this bush wasn't consumed by the fire. Moses made a decision that would change his life beyond his expectations. He said to himself, "I must turn aside and look . . ." (Exodus 3:3). It was either very good decision or a bad one, depending on your point of view, but it was a formative moment in his now troubled life. Moses had to stop and listen to learn one of the most basic lessons there is about spirituality: holy ground is not where we expect it. Holy ground is everywhere in the most ordinary places.

"When the Lord saw that he had turned aside to see, God called to him out of the bush" (Exodus 3:4). God called Moses by name, just as he does every one of us who stops to look and wonder and to be curious. God called him by name—it was personal, intimate, relational. Moses' answer was a bit cautious, I think. "And he said, "Here I am" (Exodus 3:4b). God made the moment clear: this was an extraordinary moment in an ordinary day. "Come no closer. Remove the sandals from your feet, for the place on which you are standing is holy ground" (Exodus 3:5). Just as it is when we listen to God, listen for a call from God, or are just curious about something unusual that is happening when we have ears to hear. In that moment he heard God told him the least expected words Moses ever would hear: "I will send you . . ." (Exodus 3:10).

Great news, right? You have received a call to do something big enough, worthy enough with your life. For some of us, I am sure, God gives a singular call for at least a season in life. For others of us, it isn't as direct and immediate as, "I will send you. Go now." It's just that Moses didn't see it that way. He argued with God: "Who am I?" Then, "Who are you? If they ask me your name, what will I tell them?" God gave him three answers he didn't expect to hear: "I will be with you" (Exodus 3:12). "Tell them I AM has sent me to you" (Exodus 3:14). And then God got down to the business at hand. I haven't noticed this verse before. "Go and assemble the elders of Israel. . .they will listen to your voice . . ." (Exodus 3:16).

It is one of the Bible's remarkable stories that shines a light on how God works with us. God surprised Moses and intruded on his ordinary life. God had other intentions for him. Moses didn't know it but when he listened, he encountered God *at work* for the redemption of Israel. And notice the he wasn't sent on a solo mission. He would need others at his side. Moses needed his brother, but before that partnership, God sent Moses to the elders, and others he would need from to help fulfill his mission.

In a battle with Amalek, Moses and two men, Aaron, and Hur, went to the top of a hill. Whenever Moses held up his hand, Israel prevailed in battle. When he lowered his hand, the enemy prevailed. That's when we know why Aaron and Hur were with him. "Aaron and Hur held up his hands, one on one side and the other on the other side, so his hands were steady until the sun set" (Exodus 17:12). Moses was called to mission in a singular call, however, it wasn't long before God gave him others to hold up his arms, to support, strengthen, and empower him. He was not sent into mission alone. A "leadership of companionship," it may be called. God promised Moses his presence. But God told him he would not go alone. God himself would go with him but Yahweh knew Moses needed more—he needed first the elders and Aaron, Joshua, and Hur.

You too have a sacred purpose for your life, but you cannot hold up your hands alone, without others on each side to keep you steady and strong. You have been given a sacred song, but it is not an aria or solo, it is an chorale group of musicians who together make the music of the soul available for all to experience. We listen together. We sing together. We discover what God is writing in our lives together. It is both solitary (Moses at the mountain top) and orchestral and communal (Moses and Aaron, Moses, Joshua, and Hur). Whoever wrote this story believed that we are in this spiritual work with companions, soul friends, *koinonia*. Even so, our leadership is only of the human sort. What do I mean? Dan Allender wrote a book called *Leading With a Limp*. He based it on the story of Jacob in Genesis 32, where Jacob wrestled with God and ended up "ragged, bruised, and limping." We are not alone even in the heartbreak of our human weakness—weaknesses that may be openly acknowledged or remain hidden deep within. No one is called to leadership by Yahweh simply because of great skill, strength, and power; we are called to leadership *by* Yahweh, always *with* Yahweh who goes before us, stands beside us, and has our back even as we limp in our finite humanity. Most books on leadership omit this part; Scripture does not.

> Pause for reflection: Who is your Aaron and Hur? Do you have soul friends like that? For what do you need the arms of support these men gave to Moses? For whom are you an Aaron or Hur? Sometimes we need to be for others what we need most ourselves.

There is possibly no declaration from God that blazes with such glory, power, and beauty as the sixth day of creation: "Then God said, let us make humankind in our image, according to our likeness, and let them have dominion over the fish of the seat. In the image of God, he Created *them*, male and female he created them. God blessed *them* and God said to *them*, 'Be fruitful and multiply and fill the earth and subdue it and have dominion . . .'" (Genesis 1:26–28). Now ask yourself: to whom was God speaking in this earth-shaping moment? To whom was dominion given? Who was created in God's image? The answer is breathtaking: the man (Adam) *and* the woman (Eve). *Together* they were sent into the world. *Together* they were given dominion. This is not the end of the story, but it is the beginning. Even though sin will bring trauma, damage, and punishment, God's intention was clear: he called them *together*, male and female.

Jayber Crow spoke of his town of Port William and said, "It was a community always disappointed in itself, disappointing its members, always trying to contain its divisions and gentle its meanness, always failing and yet always preserving a sort of will toward goodwill. I knew that, in the midst of all the ignorance and error, this was a membership; it was the membership of Port William and of no other place on earth."[4] Although they might not have said it like this, it seems that Jayber and Athey Keith both knew: We are formed and transformed in community. It takes ferocious resilience to enter the world of our many callings, but we are not alone. There's one more question we must ask about our sacred song: "What does community form in us?" I know the limitations of it, the disappointments, stubbornness, and even wrongheadedness we live out in the church all too often. What of the gifts it can bring? What can community form in this very human church? The answer to that in the descriptions below is nothing short of remarkable.

A THANKFUL PEOPLE

Grace leads to gratitude. I didn't know I was a curmudgeon until my friend Dan told me. I wasn't all that sure I agreed with his description but I knew one thing: his words in my life were always words of grace from which I experienced deep gratitude—for my work, my vocation, and deeply for our friendship. When you are loved, not only by Jesus, but a community of others, gratitude is a natural overflow. Gratitude is not a weapon but it can explode grace into your soul and onto those whom you thank. Gratitude releases powerful energy within your spirit. Not just words to be mumbled, but shouted with genuine gratitude.

A PEOPLE OF CONVICTION AND DISCOURSE

We arrived on an unscheduled landing on a flight into Kansas City on a wildly stormy night. To be honest, we were rattled by unpredictable air currents and turbulence and were glad to stand on terra firma. As we walked through the concourse, I noticed a young Jewish man, prayer shawl on his shoulders in a corner away from the crowds as he prayed aloud. I needed that assurance of faith that night. I needed to feel the conviction of his devotion expressed in prayer. I needed to remember Scripture's most repeated command: "Be not afraid."

---

4. Berry, *Jayber Crow*, 205.

The ancient practice that is most helpful to me apropos community is the synagogue, an innovation of the exile, some believe. In exilic life, a minyan or quorum of ten men gathered with Torah in the center of the table. Conviction was there. Torah, the law, or the instructions of Yahweh, was on the table for all to read aloud. And, what happened is instructive for us today in a bitterly divided national culture: They read Scripture and then turned to discourse—respectful debate as they argued about what the words meant. They were not in simplistic or mindless agreement on everything, they were transformed through discourse. The topic of conversation centered on the living word of God, the Torah. The protocol was discourse. Discourse recognizes there are differences of viewpoints, positions, and practices.

A PEOPLE OF *KOINONIA* (FRIENDSHIP)

Koinonia is a rich biblical understanding for who we are and what we do in the church. Sadly, it has become a forgotten word in many of our congregations. It means most simply shared participation in Christ but also refers to fellowship, and a joint or common participation in the life of the Spirit. We do that by sharing the suffering of Christ, sharing material possessions, and caring for those in need within the congregation, and serving the families, neighborhood, towns, nations, and world through our shared vocation in Jesus. We are invited to learn how to disagree with each other, set different priorities or seek a different agenda. *Koinonia* is not a formula for relationships without tensions but for truth-telling in love. Social networks in our culture can readily become spiritual networks of *koinonia*. "Your" story can be reconfigured to tell the whole story of koinonia: Y/our story. We are not in this work alone. We do not come to spiritual maturity alone. We are not only called to sacred purpose alone. Your story is also our story.

A DIVERSE PEOPLE

Tom Skinner, an African American leader, came to speak at Bethel College. Back in the day, chapel was held in the gym. He and I stood near the front and looked up at the bleachers full of an almost all-white, all-middle-class audience of students, faculty, and staff. In his introduction he referenced our conversation and said, "You know, the kingdom of God doesn't look like this." His words offended many but he spoke truth. Paul enunciated that same truth, "There is neither Jew nor Greek (nationality, race, ethnicity), slave nor free (economic and cultural identity), there is neither male nor female (gender) for you are all one in Christ" (Galatians 3:28). Is he telling us to be color-blind or culture-blind or gender-blind as if we don't recognize that we are different? No, he is ultimately saying that those distinctions will not keep us from our inheritance in Christ Jesus. It says that our ethnic, social, or gender identities are transformed by the Holy Spirit in ways that unite us as the body of Christ. Paul is teaching the church in Galatia about unity in Christ, respectful acknowledgment, and honoring of each other as created in the image of God.

When those words metabolize in your soul, it defies racism, nationalism, sexism, and all the ways we divide against one another. C. S. Lewis talked about the Dwarfs, who united against others in *The Chronicles of Narnia*. His memorably simple phrase says it clearly: "The Dwarfs are for the Dwarfs." Aslan, the Christ figure says, "You see . . .They will not let us help them. They have chosen cunning instead of belief. *Their prison is only in their own minds*, yet they are in that prison and so afraid of being taken in that they cannot be taken out" (emphasis mine).[5]

A PEOPLE TOGETHER IN FORMATION AND MISSION: WE NEED ONE ANOTHER, WE ARE NOT ALONE

The place to start is to look back over your shoulder. When you do, you remember we are not only shaped by our own identity and story. We are shaped, as well, by the story of those who preceded us, upon whose shoulders we now stand. If you are in leadership, you know you cannot claim anything other than that truth. No one succeeds in a family, neighborhood, business, church, or organization on their own.

A prayer: "God seems to put a lot of faith in flawed people like me. While I don't understand the strategy, I have found myself loved, invigorated and strangely grateful for it, at least for some followers of Jesus you have sent my way. With all the faith and courage, I have, I say 'Here I am, Lord, I will go, Lord, as you call me, where you send me, I will go.' And Yes, I will try my very hardest to hold your people in my heart, even the annoying ones."

---

5. Lewis, *Last Battle*, 707, 747, emphasis mine.

11

In the Rearview Mirror: Learning to Read Backward

You may have heard it said that vocation is a search by the young once and for all to find a single pathway and lifelong direction. I'd change that: Vocation is learning to read backward to find the way forward toward sacred purpose.

ALL THEOLOGY, LIKE ALL fiction, is at its heart autobiography.[1] So said Frederick Buechner. In the writing of autobiography, we look back and remember. We look ahead and wonder. Your particular calling is not necessarily a single moment in time that will define how you will spend all your days. I knew myself to be called to pastoral ministry in my twenties. In my thirties I found myself in a new season as a professor and pastor in a university setting. In my forties I started to write and speak broadly on Christian college campuses. In my sixties I directed a grant on the meaning of vocation, vocational discernment, and spirituality. Also, in my sixties I served God as the president of a graduate school. As my life indicates, vocation isn't necessarily a one-time decision that will lead you to a single job all your days. It may be that way for some but not for us all. Read your life as story through all the decades you are given. You may find that your

1. Buechner, *Sacred Journey*, 1.

dreams or visions for your life have changed over the years and your altars in the world are sometimes different than you expected. You may find that your heart has become softened to new and unexpected ways to write your story as the Holy Spirit focuses your eyes on different forms of purpose.

"Holding our *inner blueprint* (a good description of our soul) and returning it humbly to the world and to God by love and service is indeed of ultimate concern . . . We are here to give back fully and freely what was first given to us—but now writ personally—by us."[2] To give back is to live in compassion. Richard Foster wrote, "[God's] heart is the most sensitive and tender of all. No act goes unnoticed, no matter how insignificant or small. A cup of cold water is enough to put tears in the eyes of God. Like the proud mother who is thrilled to receive a bouquet of wilted dandelions from her child, so God celebrates our feeble expressions of gratitude."[3] Jesus said, "Be compassionate as your heavenly Father is compassionate" (Luke 6:36). God's love moves us to practice love for others.

Frederick Buechner gives two snapshots of what Jesus is after. "Compassion is the sometimes fatal capacity for feeling what it's like to live inside somebody else's skin. It is the knowledge that there can never really be any peace and joy for me until there is peace and joy finally for you too."[4] "The best moments any of us have as human beings are those moments when for a little while it is possible to escape the squirrel-cage of being *me* into the landscape of being *us*."[5]

The Scripture doesn't let us evade our daily choices: "So if you have been raised with Christ, seek the things that are above where Christ is, seated at the right hand of God. Set your minds on things that are above, not on things on earth, for you have died and your life is hidden with Christ in God . . . But now you must get rid of all such things—anger, wrath, malice, slander and abusive language from your mouth . . . Above all, clothe yourselves with love, which binds everything together in perfect harmony" (Colossians 3:1–3, 8–9, 14).

If we see others through the lens of vitriolic animus, we will in time become incapable of seeing the kingdom of God as our calling and ourselves as beloved. We become in our own story the narrative we live out with others. Some research says abused people can more readily become

2. Rohr, *Falling Upward*. 11.
3. Foster, *Prayer*, 85.
4. Buechner, *Wishful Thinking*, 15.
5. Buechner, *Wishful Thinking*, 21.

abusers themselves. When our lens are shaded and darkened by distrust or a vengeful spirit, it is a reflection of our inner spiritual state. So, Paul says, "Seek the things that are above where Christ is" (Colossians 3:1). But he then flips the script and gets real about things that exist where we live in relationships both personal and public: "As God's chosen ones, holy and beloved, clothe yourselves with compassion, kindness, humility, meekness, and patience. Bear with one another . . ."(Colossians 3:12–13). In an era when words have become increasingly violent towards others, threatening, demeaning, and strident, not to mention obscene, loud, and loveless, *what we say* and *how we say it* is a direct reflection of our inner self. "Whoever says, I abide in him (Jesus), ought to walk just as he walked." And to speak as he spoke, to love as he loved, to respect as he respected. This is the heart of all our spiritual practices.

Sometimes a writer can move readers with just a title. Brian Doyle does not have a knack for short titles, but he gets my attention. For example, he has an essay called "Furious Prayer for the Church I Love and Have Always Loved but Which Drives Me Insane with Its Fussy Fidgety Prim Tin-Eared Thirst for Control and Rules and Power and Money Rather than the One Simple Thing the Founder Insisted On." In it, he writes:

> Granted, it's a tough assignment, the original assignment. I get that. Love—Lord help us, could we not have been given something easier, like astrophysics or quantum mechanics? But no—love those you cannot love. Love those who are poor and broken and fouled and dirty and sick with sores. Love those who wish to strike you on both cheeks. Love the blowhard, the pompous ass, the arrogant liar. Find the Christ in each heart, even those. Preach the gospel and only, if necessary, talk about it. Be the Word . . . The Rabbi did not say build churches, or retreat houses or secure a fleet of cars for general use, or convene conferences or issue position papers. He was pretty blunt about the hungry and the naked and the sick. He was not reasonable: we forget this. The church is not a reasonable idea. The church should be a verb. When it is only a noun it is not what the Founder asked of us . . . Let's try again today. And so: Amen.[6]

---

6. Doyle, *Book of Uncommon Prayer*, 17–18.

AT SEVENTY, LOOKING BACK

At the occasion of his retirement, a wise friend said, "Keith, I've been redeployed. God hasn't shown me yet what's next in this new season of life, but I know that Christians aren't meant to retire. I have been redeployed." Was he still faithful to his calling in Christian higher education? He was. Was he still faithful to *Soli Deo Gloria* as his core commitment? He was. Does he know himself to be the beloved? He does. He downsized his house but not his commitment to Jesus. He is taking new directions in his seventies as he has asked the same question I have also asked in times of transition: *What's next?* The first book I ever read by Eugene Peterson pictured discipleship as *A Long Obedience in the Same Direction*. He lived that consistency as a butcher's son, a pastor, a professor, writer, and a biblical translator for *The Message*. Long obedience, a long calling, but new wineskins, fresh visions, unfolding seasons and unexpected journeys "on the way."

We tend to think of questions of vocation and sacred purpose as something necessary only for young people. On a recent "Hero of the Year" award a middle-aged veterinarian said, "As I get older I find myself more and more interested to ask the questions of purpose. Why are we here? Why am I here? What does it means to be human in all the stages of life?"[7] As we age, we are exposed to more—more perspectives, more inequities, more hypocrisy, more hope, more possibilities, and more opportunities to address questions essential to humanity: Who am I? What am I intended to do with my life? Jesus' message of the identity of belovedness and the sacred purpose of living *Soli Deo Gloria*, is for all of us, all ages.

What most of us over seventy know is that aging is a *place* of unfolding awareness. Not merely a "time" or "season" but a *place* where we practice life in both familiar and surprising new ways. Synonyms for *place* include *venue, assignment, capacity,* and *residence*. Finding my place in God's world isn't one thing but many—vocation, you have read, is spirituality or a way of being in relationship with God. It is a place where you feel "at home," and "on purpose," i.e., you have found your sacred purpose. We look back and we look ahead.

- *Retrospective*: we look back as in examen, reflecting on the day or week that is now behind us.
- *Prospective*: we look toward to the future with curiosity for hints of sacred purpose.

7. CNN Heroes.

In the Rearview Mirror: Learning to Read Backward

> Pause for reflection: *For all that has been, thanks.* Take your time and list as many things that you can remember for which you are grateful. Don't be in a hurry.

IN THE REARVIEW MIRROR: LOOKING BACK TO FIND THE WAY FORWARD

We may know God's leading best in the rearview mirror. When we look back, God's intentions for our lives begin to straighten out into something more like a clear pathway than it was when we looked ahead. *Looking ahead,* the road is often filled with obstructions, twists and turns, unseen sights and horizons not yet clear. *Looking back,* we can see how God has been present every step of the way and the road straightens out behind us. When we look back, we see something more like a clear road. It didn't look that way in my thirties or fifties. What changed? What is different? The word is *perspective.* We look in the rearview mirror and now we see that God was writing our story all along. Perspective is a way of seeing, but even more precisely, a lens through which you can view all of your life—in retrospect and prospect, looking back and looking ahead. In Latin *perspective* means "seeing through to clarity." We can say with certainty that perspective is sacramental: we see deeply enough to recognize the richest, truest meaning contained in what we have trained our lens upon. "It's just a piece of bread, it's just a cup of wine? Or is it?" You've been at a beach or mountain or your own home when someone says, "Look, do you see that?" You look everywhere they are pointing until you find their line of sight. It makes you wonder if that's why one of Jesus' repeated statements was "The kingdom of God is here, in your midst." The implication is clear: open your eyes, train your line of sight to see what Jesus saw and act on it.

"God is constantly writing our story but he (God) doesn't send us the next chapter to read in advance. Instead, we all read backward—finding the meaning in our stories as we read what God has already written. Life is a story that unfolds in such a way that we can't see very far ahead. We don't know the final outcome, or even the next plot twist, until we're in the middle of it."[8] There is no paved road to take us where we're supposed to

---

8. Allender, *To Be Told*, 101.

be—no route embedded in our GPS. Instead, we are on a journey where God gives us constantly evolving options, depending upon our choices and the choices of others as we do our best to listen to God. We each find our own way: it is not lockstep, marching in line. God is as inventive with you as with each of us. Your part is to listen and take a step forward without all the information given to you ahead of time.

In earlier years, AAA would supply step-by-step, turn-by-turn maps that told you exactly how to get to your destination. I'm convinced many of us want the same thing from God and we are disappointed that it doesn't happen as we wanted. Berry writes of Caleb, a disgruntled professor. "He is always trying to make up the difference between the life he has and the life he imagines he might have had."[9] I know people like Caleb too, but God seems to be as interested in the unexpected surprises on the journey as in knowing precisely your final destination. There were very few straight lines and fewer highways to the next destination. Thankfully I have always loved to drive the blue highways, as back roads are sometimes called, so I didn't seem to mind that my story evolved at its own pace and on a route I did not plan at the start. More often I recognized a plot only later. In college, I found a tenderness toward kids in St. Paul. Wendy and I ended up in a little inner-city church. I helped create a drop-in center that would be safer than the streets or parents too drunk or abusive or distracted to notice. And in that milieu of ministry, pain, and brokenness, I heard the echo of Grandma's voice. The pastor asked the question and I couldn't escape any longer: "Are you sure you don't have a sense of God's call to ministry?" My story had zig-zagged until I saw where the road had led all the while.

The narrative of our life is always incomplete—I think that's why God intends that we live in relationship, community, *koinonia*. We do not read it once as a finished product but more like a writer in perpetual stages of drafting and editing. I have been a doctoral advisor for friends as they worked on dissertations. Chapter by chapter is how it goes. I read the next chapter as advisor and critic. I then return it to them to reread, rewrite, and adapt the entire manuscript as it unfolds. Often the doctoral candidate will rethink the direction of an earlier chapter just as we do when we take up the discipline to read our life as story. We return to earlier chapters to understand what has emerged in more recent chapters. Our lives are not lived in a straight line with markers that say beginning, middle and end. They progress and regress, move forward and backward in what seems to

---

9. Berry, *Hannah Coulter*, 131.

be random movement. We don't always understand these movements until we look back with good questions.

The call came from Seattle, but the voice was New York Italian. I listened to his query about my interest in a dean's position. I thought he meant a dean of spiritual formation. I was mistaken. When I realized he meant the academic dean's post, Wendy heard these words from the next room, "Well, why are you calling me? I've only worked in parish and undergrad settings, I have a doctor of ministry degree, not a PhD. I'm really a spiritual formation guy with a lot of experience in higher ed." "Yes," came the voice, "That's why we're calling you." Two years later, the board asked me if I would be interested in the president's post.

Debra Rienstra, an English professor, says it poetically.

> Some people's passions are obvious and God leads them through those passions into a single path of service . . . the lifelong kindergarten teacher, or the musician who offers his skill playing every day for God's glory and other people's joy. Others, like me, have less obvious passions: what gives them energy develops over time or remains partially hidden or blooms suddenly in response to new situations. As a result, such people offer an assortment of odds and ends as service: a regular job done with integrity, some volunteer work, a career decision that seeks service over money and prestige, kindness to neighbors, maybe a late-life passion for going on mission trips or teaching teenagers appliance repair. Their lives may or may not have the clear simplicity of vocation, but at the center of everything they do is a deep love for God—and that is everyone's true vocation.
>
> I've learned that God treasures the lives made of a single piece of cloth, cut in the shape of service. But God also values the lives that look more like a bag of fabric scraps, some big pieces, some tiny pieces, different colors, and weaves. At each stage in my life, with each piece of it, I try to ask God, "How can I offer this to you?" I have to trust if I offer the odds and ends of my life, God will stitch together the pieces in some lovely pattern and receive it as my gift.[10]

Wendell Berry's character Jayber Crow has much to say about this too. Near the end of his story, he reflects on how he got to belong to Port William.

---

10. Rienstra, *So Much More*, 221–22.

Being here satisfies me. I have no thought of going away. If I knew for sure that I would die here, I would be glad. And yet definite as all this is, it seems surrounded by the indefinite, like a boat in a fog. I can't look back from where I am now and feel that I have been very much in charge of my life . . . I feel that I have lived on the edge even of my own life. I have made plans enough, but I see now that I have never lived by plan. I don't feel that I ever have been quite sure what was going on. Nearly everything that has happened to me has happened by surprise. *All* the important things have happened by surprise. And whatever has been happening usually has already happened before I had time to expect it. The world doesn't stop because you are in love or in mourning or in need of time to think. And so, when I have thought I was *in* my story or in charge of it, I really have only been on the edge of it, carried along. Is this because we are in an eternal story that is happening partly in time?[11]

This is what we can call a worthy and big enough question.

---

11. Berry, *Jayber Crow*, 322.

12

Perspective at 14,410 Feet

You may have heard it said that the future comes to those with vital vision, planning, and aggressive progress. I want to change that and say the future comes in stages to those who can say thanks and yes.

I TOOK THE INGRAHAM Glacier route to the summit of Mt. Rainer. Three of us worked well as a team and arrived at the top, exhausted but exhilarated. I took off my backpack and fell into the snow to savor the moment. Irv, our guide, stood over me with a look of utter confusion. "Keith, what are you doing?" "I'm enjoying our successful climb to the summit" was my happy answer. Irv said, "But we have not yet arrived. We are just at the edge of the Columbia crater, not the summit. We have to go down first before we reach the summit." From my perspective, we had arrived. But what lay ahead were some of the most painful and demanding steps yet. We had to descend into the crater to ascend to the summit. *Descent* is good when you are exhausted and have climbed for nearly two days to get to where you are. *Ascent* is not good when you are exhausted and have climbed for nearly two days to get to where you are. Irv encouraged me with his German accent, "One step at a time, Keith, tell yourself to raise your foot one step at a time and you'll arrive." Finally, we made it. I was cautious before I celebrated this time, but looking back, I could see the route behind us as a clear trail to the summit.

On Holy Ground

In the climbing of it, it was not clear. I could see a direction ahead but not a clear path to our goal. We had to take it step by step. Looking *back* gave me perspective to see it. Looking *back* is sometimes the only way to look ahead. It turns out we can look back with regret or disappointment. We can also look back to see gifts brought us even in our moments of disappointment.

I am still learning what started for me as a college student. I'm thinking now of the words of one of my heroes, Dag Hammarskjöld. His book *Markings* was the first book I bought as a college student that wasn't required in a class. Hammarskjöld also climbed mountains, in his native Sweden, and knew the practice required on Mt. Rainier in the depths of winter too. When the snow piles high, climbers place bamboo or wooden stakes into the ground to show where they have been, what the pathway *was* so they can find their way safely back and so others can follow as well. Those *markings* give climbers perspective and offer safety for the return. Hammarskjöld's writing was meant to be a position paper on the markings he had placed in his life—memorable thoughts, keen insights, accents of revelation, and epiphanies of glory or pain.

At one point he wrote a kind of doxology of his life. "*For all that has been, thanks, for all that will be, yes.*"[1] *For all that has been, thanks*. Not thanks because all that has happened was easy but because you are still standing and today you stand on a threshold to a portal that will take you deep into holy places. You are here in this moment and understand you have arrived in this moment because someone, the holy one of Israel, has journeyed with you to this moment—seen and unseen, heard and not, felt and not, but present. A moment to say thanks. Read it again, slowly, and let it land where it will in your present experience. Some may say immediately "it sounds naïve." For all that has been. "If you knew my story, you'd know there is brokenness in my past, experiences with the people of my narrative that have left me deeply scarred and profoundly wounded."

Hammarskjöld's words are a call to *remember* how you got to this moment in your life and to choose to live in the radicality of gratitude. "For all that has been, thanks. Thanks is not a weak declaration of naiveté but rather a fierce commitment of faith to persist and to live forward in gratitude. To say thanks, even for the pain, because we are formed in the whole of our lives, not only in the moments of sunshine, glory, and joy. To say thanks, even for the brokenness, because we are formed in the totality of our story, shaped, reshaped, formed, malformed, and reformed. To say thanks even

1. Hammarskjöld, *Markings*, 89.

for the inexplicable horrors that we have experienced because we are human persons now able to stand in solidarity with the horror of the world and the lives of people, both those we know and those we will never meet. To say thanks is a bold and courageous call to faith.

Did Hammarskjöld get it wrong? For all that has been—no, wait—some of what has been, is not a part of my life that I wish to honor. I have been abused, shamed, and hurt. And, yes, I have shamed and hurt others. Yet it is thanks for *all* that has been. Because we bring a single story forward. We may tell isolated and separate narratives that we remember in a given moment that have embedded themselves in our memory. But we are not just a compilation of our stories. We embody our whole story—or we are trying to live into that whole story. We are a story. And, pain is part of the deal. We all experience pain, loss, betrayal, harm, and abuse. We are all acquainted with disappointment, betrayal, abandonment, failure, and rejection. That is part of the deal. Wisdom is found as we learn to read the mystery in *all* of life. Our wounds are containers for sacred transformation. Hammarskjöld didn't get it wrong, after all: For all that has been, thanks.

When I wonder about my faith of the past and my feelings about the future, I head back to Port William, Kentucky to listen to Jayber Crow again. He returned to the old homestead where his adopted parents had lived.

> I sat there a long time. I looked at everything and remembered it and let my memories come back and take place. I believe I was actually thinking; my mind was too crowded and too everywhere touched. What would come, came. The child I had been came and made his motions, out and about and around, down to the store, down to the garden, down to the barn, up to the house, up to the henhouse, across the river in Uncle Othey's john boat, up the river in the buggy . . . Weaving over the ground a web of ways, as present and as passing as the spider's webs in the grass that catch the dew early in the morning . . . There had been a time before they came, and a time before that. And always, from a time before anybody knew of time, the river had been there . . . And I saw how all-of-a-piece it was, how never-ending, always coming, always there, always going . . . The world as it is would always be a reminder of the world that was and of the world that is to come.[2]

- Looking back is one way to look ahead into the future of time and beyond.

2. Berry, *Jayber Crow*, 131–32.

- Looking back reminds us that God, like that river, preceded us and will last beyond us just as God is creating all things new in the age to come.

- Looking back is one reason I persist in my faith and hope in my future, because God was there in the world that was and will be there in the world that is to come. Thank you.

My pathway has never been a direct line from point A to point B. I know people like that but they are exceptions. I have stepped off whatever good pathway I was on and got routed around to get on other good trails. I have been "a walking contradiction, partly truth and partly fiction," a fallen sinful man redeemed by Jesus, the resurrected one I seek to follow all of my days. Without the rearview mirror, I can't say I could have predicted the meandering trails of my story. But looking back I heard my name called, found my true identity, the beloved son of God, and hear it still.

AT SEVENTY, LOOKING AHEAD

I suspect most people who have not yet lived to seventy assume you spend your life at this age mostly looking back on memories, celebrating, or being haunted by them. I have not found that to be true. Instead, I see myself at seventy, still looking ahead. *"For all that will be, yes."* Someone called aging a "further journey." That rings true for my experience of seventy-plus years. What would I say to others about aging? It is surprisingly familiar and wonderfully new. And, it is an invitation to something more, something next, something further. It is not unlike what I frequently said to college students as they contemplated life after graduation. What will it be like? My answer was simply, "More." More daily tasks, chores, and rhythms, more decisions to be made, relationships to navigate, more, simply more. And less, I suppose. Health may fail, resilience will wane, strength will fade. But spirit is not dependent on physical vigor, despite what our culture says. I prefer to ask, What does God see now when I enter the room? A man defined by age? Or a beloved son in a new season of becoming?

I spent most of my professional life in a culture that never seemed to age. Students arrived in September at eighteen, left in May at twenty-one, and came again the following fall at age eighteen. Only the faculty showed signs of graying, slowing, and wrinkling. The students were always in process, seeking to forge an identity through new experiences and asking the great questions of vocation. "What's next?" is always one of life's best questions, no matter the season or the age. Beginnings occur more than once. Because I experienced moments of failure or setback, I have been gifted with new beginnings. Because I have lived through transitions, I have been gifted with new possibilities. The seasons bring us new and fresh opportunities to start again, to confirm our existing call or to listen for a new call for the coming season.

> Pause for reflection: Create a timeline: looking back, looking around today, and looking ahead. What have been defining moments for you in each of these categories, even looking ahead. To what do you feel called today? Are you being prompted to look at your vocation with fresh visions? *"For all that is yet to be, yes."* Take your time to list aspirations, dreams, and hopes for your future. To what does God seem to lead you to say, "Yes"?

Aging is only an ending if you forget the question of faith, What's next? What is the Spirit nudging us toward *in each season of life?* Perhaps the better question is what is the Spirit nudging us toward, *each day?* "The steadfast love of the Lord never ceases, his mercies never come to an end; they are new every morning; great is your faithfulness" (Lamentations 3:22–23). I find encouragement in words from the Quaker Rufus Jones: "I pin my hopes to quiet processes and small circles in which vital and transforming events take place."[3] I no longer preach to large student audiences or lead an organization as CEO. I no longer spend time with budgets and financial goals. I no longer "lead" as I once did, but I know myself to continue to be led as I always have in those past jobs. Until I reach the summit, I am not done with the journey. Until I reach the summit, I will continue to look ahead. What I know is that my story is one of many beginnings. Looking toward the future is a practice of obedient stewardship. I am asking the question of Abba Father who called me fifty years ago to a ministry that led to ordination and new ministries over the subsequent fifty years. "What is God writing in my story now? What's next?" is a question of discipleship "Lord, where can I be of help?" It is a declaration of readiness to follow Jesus. I recognize that life comes in seasons of surprise and change, not as

---

3. Jones, First Quaker World Conference.

a complete narrative of clarity and straight pathways. For students at eighteen or twenty-two, for retirees at sixty-five or seventy, the question presses for an answer. How do we read the story of vocation that God is writing in each of our life stages?

Joan Chittister asks us to look back in order to look ahead with a kind of review of life.

- Did we succeed at making the family a true family? Or being a good neighbor?
- Deep we succeed at developing a spiritual life in the presence of God?
- Did we succeed in living gently with the earth and simply learning to be happy?
- Did we succeed in developing the kind of life it takes to face the demands of life?
- Did we succeed at become a person, a person who is real?[4]

As we look backward to answer her questions, we can look forward to what might lie ahead. If you were not a good neighbor, start now. If you did not live gently with the earth, start now. Looking back, we say "thank you." Looking ahead, we say "yes, let it be." Looking ahead is what Abraham and Sarah did when God sent them to a place they did not know when they started. Like all of us. On that journey, some of us suffer chronic physical pain, others emotional and psychological trauma, and all of us, unexpected trials we didn't know how to expect and certainly didn't know how to prepare ourselves to face. I wonder if that's what the apostle James had in mind when he wrote these words for all of us: "Consider it pure joy my brothers and sisters, whenever you face trials of many kinds because you know that the testing of your faith produces perseverance. Let perseverance finish its work so that you may be mature and complete, not lacking anything" (James 1:24). My friend Wendy Delcourt wrote this in her book *Shift: Moving Toward God's Perspective*: "God uses the curriculum of pain, beauty, and awe to teach us more about this idea of heaven on earth."[5] Truly profound.

An old Hasidic saying has it that "old age is winter to the unlearned. To the wise it is harvest."[6] At dinner one evening, my wife, Wendy, observed: "Aging is like looking at a painting; it's what you choose to see, look at,

---

4. Chittister, *Gift of Years*, 115–16.
5. Delcourt, *Shift*, 30.
6. Chittister, *Gift of Years*, 85.

and focus on. You can focus on pain, aching bodies and limitations or the beauty, promise, and possibility of what is still before you. And we get to do it with a long history of seeing how God has worked to bring us to *this* time and place." With the apostle I can say again, "It's in Christ we find out who we are what we are living for. Long before we first heard of Christ, and got our hopes up, he had his eye on us, had designs on us for glorious living, part of the overall purpose he is working out in everything and everyone" (Ephesians 1:11–12, The Message). Not just at eighteen or thirty or forty-one, but all through the decades. We who have lived many decades have been given much, and so we know, therefore, that much is expected of us. Returning to a biblical view of vocation reminds us, our story is not yet complete, our vocation is not ended if we retire. Rather, we are redeployed.

> The truth, I have come to think, is that there is no such thing as having only one life to live, the fact is that every life is simply a series of lives, each one of them with its own task, its own flavor, its own brand of errors, its own type of sins, its own glories, its own kind of deep, dank despair, its own plethora of possibilities, all designed to lead us to the same end—happiness and a sense of fulfillment. Life is a mosaic made of multiple pieces, each of them full in itself, each of them a stepping stone on the way to the rest of it ... Each of them makes us new. And each of them has a purpose.[7]

I am not content to only look backward. I still look to a future God will reveal. There are longings, regrets, unfulfilled dreams, unresolved conflicts, and pain to be endured—of that I am sure. That too is what aging has become for me at times. Not bitterness or enormous loss but awareness that when I am finished with time, I will still want more ... more time to complete, fix, resolve, or simply experience more. I am not yet content to die and be finished: the reason I hold my faith with such ferocity is that I believe in my bones that resurrection is more real than all that is, that when my body says, "It is finished," my spirit will just be getting started.

POSTCARDS FROM THE FUTURE

I give good gifts. It is itself a gift I have. Benjamin, our first-born grandson, graduated high school and left for a two-year program that equipped him to become a firefighter and EMT. We gave him a check because good grandparents always give money. I also gave him a baseball signed by the

---

7. Chittister, *Gift of Years*, xii.

On Holy Ground

Cubs World Series star Kris Bryant, whose jersey I wear when I watch Cubs games. I gave him a water cannon squirt gun that shoots seventy feet as a means of stress relief. I gave him two, one for himself and the other for his roommate, just to keep it fair. I made a deal with Josh, the roommate, who agreed to blast Benjamin from a hiding place to start a summer of water attacks. But I also asked my son-in-law, a firefighter, what piece of equipment would have meaning for Benjamin. There is a belt a firefighter wears around their coat that holds the radio—the source of survival in a burning building, for victims and for firefighters. A radio can save a life. Another firefighter at my son-in-law's station handcrafts such belts and hand-tools them with the name of the station house (in this case, Black Butte, OR) and the name of the firefighter (Benjamin Carl White).

We had a family gift-giving time but no one was prepared for what was to come. I told Benjamin the story of how the belt came to be and he dropped his head and said nothing for almost ten minutes. He choked back his tears and looked at this symbol of his chosen calling, his future and his journey into adulthood. We had the sense as a family to let the moment bring all the emotions it needed. He told us later he saw it as a symbol of leaving childhood behind. He enjoyed it as he looked ahead to the future he believes God has called him to. "I was born for this," he said to his grandmother. We finished the evening by laying hands on him and prayed for him, celebrated his graduation and his future.

Looking back is one our greatest gifts as we age. We can see generations past and generations future. As we give good gifts, we are, at the same time, receiving the gift of glimpses into tomorrow, *postcards from the future*. They call us to fidelity to both God's gifts and the needs of the world. While I may look back on seasons of my own life, I look forward to these postcards from the future that will be written by God's pen in the lives of my children and grandchildren. "*For all that has been, thanks. For all that is yet to come, yes.*"

Jan Richardson has written a blessing that is a benediction for all that you have read. Her poetic honesty is breathtaking.

> This blessing
> is for the moment
> after clarity has come,
> after inspiration,
> after you have agreed
> to what seems
> impossible.

Perspective at 14,410 Feet

This blessing
is what follows
after illumination departs
and you realize
there is no map
for the path
you have chosen,
no one to serve
as guide,
nothing to do
but gather up
your gumption
and set out.

This blessing
will go with you.
It carries no answers,
no charts,
no plans.

It carries no source
of light
within itself.

But in its pocket
is tucked a mirror
that, from time to time,
it will hold up to you

to remind you
of the radiance
that came when you gave
your awful and wondrous *yes*.[8]

---

8. Richardson, *Circle of Grace*, 51–52.

A Word After: What's Next?

BRENNAN MANNING WROTE *The Ragamuffin Gospel* for those not sure what to think about their identity or whether they even had a relationship with God. He summarized his book with a simple statement: "The Bible is a love story of God with His people. God calls, pursues, forgives and heals. Our response to His love is itself His gift."[1] Jesus did not teach about careers, occupations, retirement, or finding your life's itinerary. But the Scriptures teach something too deeply important to overlook: God is one who calls. God sees you as beloved and will show the way to find your sacred purpose through loving companionship.

What's next? By now it might be clear: read your life as story: return to the holy ground of your own vocation. Read it to discover how to live with sacred purpose. Read carefully enough that you may go deep below the surface to discover pathways to take. Listen for God's intentions for the world and then ask the deep questions all over again. As you read your story, pay attention to the distinctives of face, race, place, and grace. Listen to the shadows, darkness, failures, heartbreaks, and shipwrecks of your life for what they reveal about your identity in Christ. You may find there clues, hints, nudges, or taps on the shoulder from Jesus. Listen in community with others, soul friends, for the sake of others, and you will find the world's great needs as they offer additional clues, hints, or even a summons to where God intends for you to serve. And, continue to listen in all the seasons your story told: listen for fresh visions or "new wineskins," for something "next" that God might be calling you through your life of kingdom choices.

As I age, I can readily look back but my understanding of my story as vocation asks me, What's next? What might God intend for me and a lot of

---

1. Manning, *Ragamuffin Gospel*, 201.

us whose voices have a long history of seeking to follow God with fidelity? Yes, we have failed and have worn what Brennan called "Tilted Halos."[2] We have learned to walk with a limp because our choices have sometimes caused us to trip, slip, and fall. We have listened to our own imposter and false self and discovered ourselves in need of grace, repentance, and redemption, but we also bring rich experience in realigning our lives in the most foundational ways possible.

As I have noted, Brennan was one of my most necessary teachers. I didn't discover Brennan's work until I was in my forties. Why Brennan? Because in one sentence he could speak truth in ways that got your attention and leave you a bit bruised; in the next sentence he could touch your soul with grace as tender as the touch of Jesus. What would he say to us at this stage in our exploration? He would tell us, "Say yes to what you sense as that nudge, whisper, touch, or summons from the story as God is writing it." It is not in the past tense, as if God wrote your story once and then let it be. More than anyone in my life, Brennan helped me feel, not just "think" or "believe" in my identity as the beloved of God. He showed me that love again and again in conversations and phone calls. His radical belief in our identity as the beloved transformed me, healed me, and restored me—not with guilt and shame (guilt means I did something bad, shame means "I am bad")—but as the gospel always seems to—with grace. John wrote, "God didn't go to all the trouble of sending his Son merely to point an accusing finger, telling the world how bad it was. He came to help, to put the world right again" (John 3:15–16, The Message).

Identity leads to vocation, do you see it? Because you see God differently, now you can see yourself differently and everyone you encounter becomes an opportunity to do for others what God has done for you— loved you. Period. Vocation as a lifelong companionship with Abba is not simplistic rhetoric, it is theologically grounded truth. God relates to us with grace and surprising, relentless love.

What trips us up, many times over, is panic. I need to make a decision about this job by Monday morning. I have a deadline decision that is stressing me out. And I would want to know—how are you doing in your response to the primary call of God on all your life? How have you practiced listening in prayer, to Scripture and to wise friends? How have you listened to your, life, all of it? How have you listened with the rest of the orchestra with whom your life will offer the most remarkable music? To your panic,

---

2. Manning, *Ragamuffin Gospel*, 72.

On Holy Ground

I would simply say, "There is no panic in Jesus." There is a radical form of trustful listening. Jesus taught us that your story is being written in your most ordinary moments, your most painful moments, your moments of greatest failure and your greatest moments of greatest fidelity, when you have said yes.

Hear it again: "Define yourself radically as one beloved of God."[3] And then boldly, prayerfully, choose you this day, *how* you will serve the one who calls you beloved. Say yes, say no, make the move now, wait, look at other options, research your choices and consider what you know of the story of the gospel and God's intentions, your sacred design, all your story including the story of community, and make your choice. If it turns out wrong, make your choice again. No one promised this would be without messiness, did they? You are loved by God. Remember? "Love is patient; love is kind . . . It bears all things, believes all things, hopes all things, endures all things . . . Now we see in a mirror, dimly, but then we shall see face to face. Now I know only in part; then I will know fully, even as I have been fully known. And now faith, hope, and love abide, these three; and the greatest of these is love" (1 Corinthians 13:4, 7, 12–13).

Even as you consider something new or "next," be faithful to your vocation by doing ably the things you already know you have been called to do. Faithfulness is the portal through which your heart stretches towards resilience and compassion. Resilience, because a pliable, receptive heart becomes strong through faithfulness. Compassion, because an open, joyful, and receptive heart cannot help but see opportunities to show compassion toward others. "To follow Jesus means that we can't separate what Jesus is saying from what Jesus is doing and the way that he is doing it. To follow Jesus is as much, or maybe even more, about feet as it is about ears and eyes."[4]

"You are a chosen people, a royal priesthood, a holy nation, a people belonging to God, that you may declare the praises of darkness into his wonderful light. Once you were not a people but now you are the people of God . . ." (1 Peter 2:9–10). "A Christian is one who is on the way, though not necessarily very far along it, and who has at least some dim and half-baked idea of whom to thank."[5] It is a place to begin.

---

3. Manning, *Abba's Child*, 59.
4. Peterson, *Run with the Horses*, 22.
5. Buechner, *Wishful Thinking*, 14.

Appendix

THE VOCARE WORKSHEET, INCLUDED below, was developed in response to mentees and students who asked for a practical tool to help discern their calling or vocation. *On Holy Ground* argues that simply learning to read one's own life story is not enough to full engage with the biblical teachings on calling. The worksheet incorporates four key themes: The Gospel Story, Your Sacred Design, Your Sacred Song, and Your Life of Kingdom Choices.

On Holy Ground

The Vocare Worksheet: Your Sacred Story: Identity, compassion, sacred purpose.

THE GOSPEL STORY: Read God's intentions for the world…	YOUR SACRED DESIGN: Read your life as story…	OUR SACRED SONG: Read your story with and for the sake of others…
<ul><li>To know God's heart in robust, disciplined study of Scripture.</li><li>To recognize the nature and character of God as you discover what God is doing in time and space, ie what matters to God in the present moment.</li><li>To focus your life as missional so you identify *why you serve* within world and church.</li><li>To center your life in alignment with Biblical, theological, and cultural awareness of God at work in the world.</li><li>To focus your life around biblical priorities</li><li>To find your voice and practice of compassion in our divided culture.</li></ul>	<ul><li>To discern your sacred design through all the things that shape your identity as *imago dei* (the image of God), face, race, place, and grace.</li><li>To find meaning in the emerging story of brokenness and grace in our lives.</li><li>To identity both natural and nurtured talents.</li><li>To identify your Charism(s) (spiritual gifting).</li><li>To recognize social and cultural factors in your story in time and place.</li><li>To know yourself as the beloved of God as you identity gifts, capacities, and strengths.</li></ul>	<ul><li>To see how God works through collaboration, partnership, & theological hospitality.</li><li>To discern *how* you uniquely inhabit the world including organizations you serve.</li><li>To discern *how* you are shaped and misshaped in/by others.</li><li>To discern that you serve Jesus *for the sake of others.*</li><li>To enable you to find your way of being in job, family, community, church, relationships, and koinonia.</li><li>To discern your unique purpose and place in God's world *with others*.</li></ul>
Discover God's priorities for the world and your sacred purpose	Discover your God-given identity: who you are in time and space	Discover sacred purpose in community for the sake of others

Vocare: your never changing, meta life-calling: to live all to the glory of God: *Soli Deo Gloria*

Created in the image of God (*imago dei*), your God-given identity is as the beloved of God, living in the presence of Abba Father, *Coram Deo.*

YOUR LIFE OF KINGDOM CHOICES: Read your life as story in all seasons of life.

To find your emerging place in God's kingdom in unfolding seasons of life.	To recognize that Vocation is comprised of many directions taken over a lifetime.
To say thanks for what has been and yes to what is ahead	In order to faithfully seek fresh vision in your lifelong commitment to live with sacred purpose.
To see God has lead you in retrospect and anticipate where you will be led in the future.	In order to practice sacred purpose at your many altars in the world
To discern your life as holy pilgrimage with sacred purpose	In order to commit your life to following Jesus in compassion

Discover that vocation is a spirituality of lifelong companionship with Abba.

Bibliography

Adichie, Chimamanda Ngozi. "The Danger of a Single Story." https://www.ted.com/talks/chimamanda_ngozi_adichie_the_danger_of_a_single_story?language=en.
Allender, Dan. *The Hidden Hope of Lament.* https://theallendercenter.org/2016/06/hidden-hope-lament.
———. *Leading With a Limp: Take Full Advantage of Your Most Powerful Weakness.* Colorado Springs: Waterbrook, 2008
———. *A Spirituality of Listening.* Downers Grove, IL: InterVarsity, 2016.
———. *To Be Told: God Invites You to Coauthor Your Future.* Colorado Springs: Waterbrook, 2005.
———. "Understanding Your Story." https://www.andsonsmagazine.com/07.
Anderson, Keith R., and Randy Reese. *Spiritual Mentoring: A Guide for Seeking and Giving Direction.* Downers Grove, IL: InterVarsity, 1999.
Aristedes. *The Apology of Aristedes on Behalf of Christians.* Piscataway, NJ: Gorgias, 2004.
Bailey, Kenneth. *Jesus Through Middle Eastern Eyes.* London: SPCK, 2008.
Barclay, William. Greek Word Studies 2564, *Kaleo.* Audio recording. https://www.sermonindex.net/modules/articles/index.php?view=article&aid=33666#.
Barry, William. *God's Passionate Desire and Our Response.* Notre Dame, IN: Ave Maria, 1992.
Berry, Wendell. "Christianity and the Survival of Creation." *CrossCurrents,* 43.2 (Summer 1993).
———. *Hannah Coulter.* Berkeley, CA: Counterpoint, 2004.
———. "Health Is Membership." Audio recording. Delivered at the conference "Spirituality and Healing," October 17, 1994.
———. *Jayber Crow: The Life Story of Jayber Crow, Barber of the Port William Membership as Written by Himself.* Washington, DC: Counterpoint, 2000.
———. *A Place in Time.* Berkeley, CA: Counterpoint, 2012.
———. *Standing by Words.* Berkeley, CA: Counterpoint, 2011.
Bono. US National Prayer Breakfast, 2006. https://www.americanrhetoric.com/speeches/bononationalprayerbreakfast.htm.
Brueggemann, Walter. *The Bible Makes Sense.* Cincinnati: St. Anthony Messenger, 2003.
———. *Theology of the Old Testament.* Minneapolis: Fortress, 1997.
Buechner, Frederick. *Listening to Your Life.* New York: Harper Collins, 1992.

Bibliography

———. *Now and Then: A Memoir of Vocation*. San Francisco: HarperSanFrancisco, 1983.
———. *A Room Called Remember*. San Francisco: Harper & Row, 1984.
———. *The Sacred Journey*. New York: Harper & Row, 1982.
———. *Wishful Thinking: A Theological ABC*. New York: Harper & Row, 1973.
Burridge, Richard A. *Imitating Christ: An Inclusive approach to New Testament Ethics*. Grand Rapids: Eerdmans, 2007.
Canlis, Julie. "The Incarnation is the Rule, not the Exception." *Christianity Today*, December, 2018. https://www.christianitytoday.com/women/2018/december/chirstmas-advent-incarnation-is-the-rule-not-exception.html.
———. *A Theology of the Ordinary*. Wenathchee, WA: Godspeed, 2017.
Canlis, Julie, and Matt Canlis. *Godspeed: The Pace of Being Known*. https://www.livegodspeed.org/watchgodspeed.
Chittister, Joan. *The Gift of Years: Growing Older Gracefully*. New York: BlueBridge, 2008.
CNN Heroes. https://www.cnn.com/videos/tv/2023.12.12.cnnheroes-tribute-hoty-dwane-stewart.cnn.
Cohen, Leonard. "Anthem." Track 5, *The Future*. New York: Columbia Records, 1992.
De Caussade, Jean Pierre. *The Sacrament of the Present Moment*. New York: HarperCollins, 1981.
Delcourt, Wendy. *Shift: Moving Toward God's Perspective*. Sisters, OR: Deep River, 2021.
Dillard, Annie. *The Writing Life*. New York: Harper Perennial, 1989.
Doperbeck, David. *Barth Through a Glass Darkly*. https://davidopderbeck.com/tgdarkly/2020/07/14/barth-on-the-free-theologian/.
Doyle, Brian. *A Book of Uncommon Prayer: 100 Celebrations of the Miracle and Muddle of the Ordinary*. Notre Dame, IN: Sorin, 2014.
Finley, James. *Merton's Palace of Nowhere*. Notre Dame, IN: Ave Maria, 1978.
Foster, Richard. *Prayer: Finding the Heart's True Home*. San Francisco: Harper, 1992.
Godwin, Gail. *Evensong*. New York: Ballantine, 1999.
Gorman, Amanda. *Call Us What We Carry*. New York: Viking, 2021.
Guinness, Os. *The Call*. Nashville: Thomas Nelson, 1998.
Hammarskjöld, Dag. *Markings*. New York: Alfred A. Knopf, 1968.
Heschel, Abraham Joshua. *God in Search of Man*. New York: The Noonday Press/Farrar, Straus and Giroux, 1983.
Jones, Dawson, and Laurel Jones. *Finding God in the Geography of our Hearts, A Year Later*. blog, 2021. https://dawsonandlaurel.com/blog/.
Jones, Rufus. First Quaker World Conference, 1937. https://qfp.quaker.org.uk/passage/24–56/.
Keller, Tim. *Redefining Work*. https://www.youtube.com/watch?v=fGH5bhUwMB4.
Kelley, Thomas. *A Testament of Devotion*. New York: HarperCollins, 1996.
Lamott, Anne. *Help, Thanks, Wow: The Three Essential Prayers*. New York: Riverhead, 2012.
———. *Stitches: A Handbook on Meaning, Hope & Repair*. New York: Riverhead, 2013.
Lawrence (Brother). *The Practice of the Presence of God*. New York: Fleming H. Revell, 1895.
Lewis, C. S. *The Chronicles of Narnia: The Last Battle*. New York: HarperCollins, 1982.
Lonergan, Bernard. "Growing in Faith as the Eyes of Being in Love with God." YouTube. https://www.youtube.com/watch?v=Q8lkKWYCyz8.
Luther, Martin. *Kritische Gesamtausgab*. In *Werke*, vol 14. Stuttgart: Verlag Hermann Böhlhaus, Nachf, 1883–2009.

Bibliography

Manning, Brennan. *Abba's Child: The Cry of the Heart for Intimate Belonging*. Colorado Springs: NavPress, 1994.

———. *The Importance of Being Foolish: How to Think Like Jesus*. San Francisco: HarperSanFrancisco, 2005

———. *Ragamuffin Gospel*. Sisters, OR: Multnomah, 2000.

Merton, Thomas. *The Hidden Ground of Love: Letters*. New York: Farrar, Straus, Giroux, 1985.

———. *New Seeds of Contemplation*. New York: New Directions, 1961.

Moltmann, Jürgen. *The Crucified God*. London: SCM, 1974.

Nigro, Nicholas, ed. *The Spirituality of Bono*. Milwaukee: Backbeat, 2014.

Nouwen, Henri. "Finding Our Sacred Center." 2014. https://www.youtube.com/watch?v=mn-UOjzwcBs.

———. *In the Name of Jesus: Reflections on Christian Leadership*. New York: Crossroad, 1989.

———. *Life of the Beloved*. New York: Crossroad, 1992.

———. *Making All Things New: An Invitation to the Spiritual Life*. San Francisco: HarperSanFrancisco, 1981.

———. *Wisdom for the Long Walk of Faith*. New York: HarperOne, 2015.

———. *With Burning Hearts: A Meditation on the Eucharistic Life*. Maryknoll, NY: Orbis, 2012.

———. "You Belong to God." https://henrinouwen.org/meditations/you-belong-to-God-2.

Ogilvie, Lloyd. "Senate Chaplain's Prayers Are Brief but Memorable." May 3, 2002. https://layman.org/newsbe44/.

Oliver, Mary. *New and Selected Poems*. Boston: Beacon, 1992.

Palmer, Parker. *The Courage to Teach: Exploring the Inner Landscape of a Teacher's Life*. San Francisco: Jossey-Bass, 1988.

———. *Let Your Life Speak: Listening for the Voice of Vocation*. San Francisco: Jossey-Bass, 2000.

Parks, Sharon Daloz. *Big Questions, Worthy Dreams: Mentoring Emerging Adults in Their Search for Meaning, Purpose, and Faith*. San Francisco: Jossey-Bass, 2000.

Peacore, Linda. "Vocation and the Christian Life." *Fuller Magazine*. https://www.fuller.edu/next-faithful-step/classes/cf565/vocation-and-the-christian-life/#:~:text=It%20is%20a%20call%20to,the%20whole%20of%20everyday%20life.

Peterson, Eugene. *As Kingfishers Catch Fire*. Colorado Springs: Waterbrook, 2017.

———. *Christ Plays in Ten Thousand Places: A Conversation in Spiritual Theology*. Grand Rapids: Eerdmans, 2008.

———. *A Long Obedience in the Same Direction*. Downers Grove, IL: InterVarsity, 1980.

———. "Missing Ingredient: Why Spirituality Needs Jesus." *The Christian Century*, March 22, 2023. https://www.christiancentury.org/article/2003-03/missing-ingredient.

———. *Run with the Horses*. Downers Grove, IL: InterVarsity, 1983.

Rienstra, Debra. *So Much More: An Invitation to Christian Spirituality*. San Francisco: Jossey-Bass, 2005.

Richardson, Jan. *Circle of Grace*. Orlando, FL: Wanton Gospeller, 2015.

Rohr, Richard. *Falling Upward*. San Francisco: Jossey-Bass, 2011.

———. *True Self, False Self*. Audio CD. Cincinnati, OH: Franciscan Media, 2003.

Rutledge, Fleming. *Means of Grace*. Grand Rapids: Eerdmans, 2021.

Ryan, William P. *Working from the Heart*. New York: Jason Araonson, 2011.

Bibliography

Sayers, Dorothy. *Creed or Chaos*. New York: Harcourt & Brace, 1949.

Sellner, Edward C. "Soul Friendship in Early Celtic Monasticism." https://www.aisling.com/aislingmagazine/articles/TAM17/friendship.html.

Shapiro, Rami. *Wisdom of the Jewish Sages: A Modern Reading of Pirke Avot*. https://www.spiritualityandpractice.com/book-reviews/view/5600/wisdom-of-the-jewish-sages.

Spitzer, Toba. *Tzedek: The Jewish Value of Justice*. https://www.myjewishlearning.com/article/tzedek-the-jewish-value-of-justice/.

Sproul, R. C. "What Does Coram Deo Mean?" https://www.ligonier.org/blog/what-does-coram-deo-mean.

Taylor, Barbara Brown. *An Altar in the World: A Geography of Faith*. New York: HarperCollins, 2010.

———. *Gospel Medicine,* Boston: Cowley, 1995.

———. *Home by Another Way*. Boston: Cowley, 1999.

———. *The Preaching Life*. Boston: Cowley, 1993.

Thibodeaux, Mark E. *Re-Imaging the Ignatian Examen: Fresh Ways to Pray from Your Day*. Chicago: Loyola, 2015.

Thompson, Curt. *The Soul of Shame*. Downers Grove, IL: InterVarsity, 2015.

Thrasher, Travis. *Bono: From the Sheer Face of Love*. Audio CD. Grand Rapids: Zondervan Brilliance, 2021.

Thurman, Howard. *Jesus and the Disinherited*. Richmond, IN: Abingdon, 1976.

Touré, Y. Itihari. *Ritual is a Means of Remembering the Human Spirit*. 2024. www.wabashcenter.wabash.edu/2024/01/ritual-is-a-means-of-remembering-the-human-spirit/.

Tutu, Desmond. *An African Prayer Book*. New York: Doubleday, 1995.

Warren, Tish Harrison. *Liturgy of the Ordinary: Sacred Practices in Everyday Life*. Downers Grove, IL: InterVarsity, 2000.

Willard, Dallas. *The Divine Conspiracy: Rediscovering Our Hidden Life in God*. New York: HarperCollins, 1998.

———. "Spirituality Made Hard." https://dwillard.org/articles/spirituality-made-hard.interview129.

Wooden, John. "The True Test of a Man's Character." https://www.goodreads.com/quotes/203719-the-true-test-of-a-man-s-character-is-what-he.

Wright, N. T. *Reflecting the Glory*. Minneapolis: Augsburg, 1998.

www.ingramcontent.com/pod-product-compliance
Lightning Source LLC
Chambersburg PA
CBHW020854160426
43192CB00007B/920